THE COMPASSION OF THE FATHER

THE COMPASSION OF THE FATHER

BORIS BOBRINSKOY

Translated by
ANTHONY P. GYTHIEL

Introduction by
MAXIME EGGER

ST VLADIMIR'S SEMINARY PRESS
CRESTWOOD, NEW YORK 10707
2003

Library of Congress Cataloging-in-Publication Data

Bobrinskoy, Boris.
    [Compassion du Père. English]
    The Compassion of the Father / by Boris Bobrinskoy ; translated by
Anthony P. Gythiel ; introduction by Maxime Egger.
        p. cm
    Includes bibliographical references and index.
    ISBN 0–88141–251–1
    1. Spiritual life—Orthodox Eastern Church.   I. Title.
BX382.B6313 2003
230'.19—dc21

                                                            2003049819

THE COMPASSION OF THE FATHER

ST VLADIMIR'S SEMINARY PRESS
575 Scarsdale Rd., Crestwood, NY 10707
1–800–204–2665

First published in French in 2000
under the title *La compassion du Père*
by Editions du Cerf

ISBN 0–88141–251–1

CONTENTS

Introduction

Facing Evil and Suffering

The Liturgy of the Heart

Toward the Knowledge of God

TOWARD A TRANSPARENCY TO THE HOLY TRINITY: THE LIFE AND WORK OF FATHER BORIS BOBRINSKOY

"For the Lamb at the center of the throne will be their shepherd; He will lead them to springs of living water. And God will wipe away every tear from their eyes." (Rev 7:17)

Life and Spiritual Journey

In a triumphant proclamation of the human will and the sovereignty of human beings as masters of their fate, André Malraux wrote, "Man is what he makes of himself." The life experience of Father Boris Bobrinskoy presents the opposite side of this self-deifying logic: the human being is not autonomous and self-defining—neither master of the mystery of being nor of becoming. Created in the image of God, the human being is "programmed" by the baptismal gift of the Holy Spirit and gradually is "created" by others—not only biologically, but also spiritually and intellectually. Only by completing this "program of grace" and by entering into this "spiritual filiation" may a person achieve his or her freedom.

A human being does not create himself or herself from nothingness. There is a development in relation to others, on the basis of what fathers, mothers, and others impart to him or her. Paradoxically, the uniqueness of the person is shaped within a tradition, through links with people, present and past, which are living memories. Every person is an heir, a creature of God destined to become a "son" or a "daughter" and, in turn, a "father" or a "mother." The existential and spiritual journey of Fr Bobrinskoy is an admirable illustration of this process. His formation and development are deeply indebted to all those who have been his "fathers in the faith" to one degree or another, and he gives unceasing thanks to God for them.

A Childhood with the Jesuits

Like many of their compatriots, the Bobrinskoys—a noble family from St Petersburg, whose family tree dates back to the end of the eighteenth century—left Russia in 1917, at the time of the Bolshevik revolution. After passing through several countries, they settled in Paris. It is there that Boris Bobrinskoy was born in 1925. The youngest of the family—he has four brothers and sisters—his childhood was marked in particular by a tragic event: the death of his mother when he was barely ten years old. This was a true upheaval, inwardly and outwardly.

His father placed him in a boarding school to help Russian children, founded in 1925 by the Belgian province of the Society of Jesus. There he received a basic French-Russian education, which he remembers fondly: "And thus I did my core secondary studies at Namur and in Paris, in Jesuit schools, up to the baccalaureate. These Jesuit Fathers, who belonged to the Eastern Rite themselves, made us speak Russian and attend the Byzantine Liturgy in the morning, where I chanted. I am very grateful to them, and especially to some of them, for having strengthened me in my priestly vocation."[1]

Indeed, from the age of eight, Fr Boris has had, by his own admission, "the very concrete desire, somewhat irrational but nonetheless precise and well defined, to become a priest," a deep, intimate conviction without any other justification. "Of course, I did not have the faintest idea of what all this might mean, but I loved the liturgical celebrations. A priest, Fr Ioann Tsaritelly had noticed me. He visited the

---

[1]All nonreferenced quotations are from a 1999 interview with Fr Boris Bobrinskoy in Paris.

houses of Russian children in the Atlantic Pyrénées, where I spent the summers and winters between the ages of seven and twelve. He came every Thursday to teach us catechism, say a prayer, and sometimes celebrate the Liturgy. I befriended him at once, and he represented for me a type of exemplary figure, of an affective fixation. Joy and seriousness radiated from him. He succeeded in imparting to me a sense of the sacred, a respect for the house of God."

This precocious vocation, of which his father disapproved but in which his mother secretly delighted, was never to leave him, nor would it ever be questioned. It was an inward compass that would allow him to keep on course: in the natural tempest of adolescence, in the crises and sufferings of a bereaved, orphaned soul moving around from boarding school to boarding school, and within the difficult relationship with a faraway, absent father. "This inward evidence of a vocation prevented me from getting lost or being overwhelmed. It permitted these years, which were not always easy, to become a time of spiritual sowing."

At the same time as this formation with the Jesuits, Fr Boris and some of his young friends created and developed bonds with the Orthodox Church, particularly the Russian ecclesial circles in Paris. During the entire war he served as an acolyte at the St Alexander Nevsky Cathedral on Daru Street. In 1942, he chose as his spiritual director Fr Cyprian Kern, professor at St Sergius, the Orthodox Institute of Theology.

Studies at the St Sergius Institute

In 1944, after obtaining the baccalaureate, Fr Boris quite naturally entered the St Sergius Institute. He at once became integrated into this environment marked by the Russian language and tradition, immersing himself totally into its liturgical and spiritual life. This was a "heroic" time. During the war, the institute managed to survive almost miraculously, despite great difficulties. Aid coming from England, America, Sweden, Switzerland, and the Ecumenical Council of Churches (COE) was interrupted because of the hostilities. In addition, as a former property of a German Lutheran community, St Sergius almost was taken over by the Gestapo during the occupation. The material situation was catastrophic: salaries were not paid, food was insufficient, and the students—about twenty, initially all Russians—managed as well as they could, thanks to small, extra jobs. There was no heating, except for some primitive sawdust stoves, and the winter was harsh. "I remember that it was very cold. The first winter, I had terrible chilblains. As I preferred buying books instead of food with the little money I had received as a grant, I fell ill and I lost a year."

However, as much as St Sergius was cold externally, internally it was living and rich. The moment Fr Boris entered (at the same time as the future, renowned theologian John Meyendorff) right after the Liberation, corresponded to an authentic renewal. Fr Sergius Bulgakov had just passed away, but most of the professors who were its glory before the war were still teaching there: Antony Kartachev, Basil Zenkovski, Leon Zander, Msgr Cassien, the Fathers Nicholas Afanasiev, Cyprian Kern, and Georges Florovsky. Father Alexander Schmemann, then a deacon, also had begun to work there. He was to play an important role in the rediscovery of the liturgical and eucharistic dimension of the Church and in the development of a renewed vision of its history. "All these personalities have evidently made an impression upon me. More notably, I owe a great deal to Fr Sergius Bulgakov, whose spirit was still very present at St Sergius. Whatever we may think of his sophiological concepts (after an initial movement of enthusiasm, I removed myself from them rather quickly) we should acknowledge that his theological thought, nourished by its liturgical sources, was very alive and thought-provoking."

Fr Boris presented a vibrant homage to Fr Bulgakov, whom he characterized as a "visionary of wisdom," on occasion of the fiftieth anniversary of his death. Having emphasized his "flamboyant presence" and his "theological genius," he concluded, "The moment will come—will we be its creators or even its witnesses?—when, with the subsiding of time and of the passions, the Church will welcome lovingly the testimony of the life and faith of Fr Sergius, eliminating from his doctrine its ambiguities of errors, and praising his spiritual authenticity, his fervent love of the Church, his certainty drawn from the depth of the eucharistic chalice, that the kingdom of God is at hand, that the Lord is coming."[2]

Although he was a *persona non grata* at St Sergius because of the active role he played in the condemnation of Fr Sergius Bulgakov and of his sophiology by the Patriarchate of Moscow in the mid 1930s, Vladimir Lossky also influenced Fr Boris at the beginning of his studies. "The discovery of his masterpiece *Mystical Theology of the Eastern Church* was a surprise. I became his friend and a friend of the family quite rapidly."

Thus, Palamite theology and all of neopatristic thought, also advocated by Fr Georges Florovsky, would gradually enter the theological and spiritual horizon of Fr Boris. This movement of patristic renewal developed forcefully, in particular with the publication of the collection *Sources chrétiennes.* It regrouped personalities such as Fr Paul Henry, specialist in Plotinus and St Augustine, Fr Henri de Lubac, author of remarkable studies on Origen and the Church, and the future cardinal Jean Daniélou whose masterpiece *Platonisme et théologie mystique* made a deep impression upon him. "It is through him notably that I discovered the Cappadocian Fathers, in particular Gregory of Nyssa, the reading of whom has affected me greatly."

This "patristic renaissance," this time of a biblical return to the sources and of a liturgical renewal, was especially strong in the Catholic Church through the German abbey of Maria Laach (Dom Odo Casel) and in Anglicanism. *The Shape of the Liturgy* by Dom Gregory Dix, a large fresco on the evolution of the liturgy from its beginnings, animated by a powerful breath and vision, became a favorite bedside book of Fr Boris.

He was also among the young theologians who gathered around Fr Alexander Schmemann for fascinating and impassioned exchanges, particularly inside the small Fraternity of Christ the Savior. "We convened to discuss theological and ecclesial problems . . . I still

[2]"Le père Serge Boulgakov," *Supplement au SOP (Service Orthodoxe de Presse)* no. 196 (March 1995) 1920.

remember these somewhat Homeric debates and these disputes between Fr Alexander, who advocated some type of liturgical and eucharistic maximalism, and the followers of a more traditional approach. These discussions were very useful; they helped us deepen our own experience and orient ourselves gradually."

St Sergius provided a living and nourishing environment for budding theologians opening themselves to the life of the Spirit, to the Scriptures, to the church fathers, and to the Liturgy. "While thinking about it again, it was indeed a quite extraordinary time, a unique moment of renewal, of convergence between biblical, liturgical, and patristic theology, with a truly ecumenical openness, animated by a sincere desire to return to the sources, a search to overcome the divisions among Christians by going back as far as possible to rediscover the common trunk of the one Church of the East and the West."

Fr Boris ended his theological studies in 1949. He wrote a thesis on the sacrament of chrismation in the Syro-Palestinian tradition of the fourth century, researching authors such as Cyril of Jerusalem, Ephrem the Syrian, and St John Chrysostom. He discovered that chrismation then was celebrated not after baptism, but before. Thus, there was a pre-baptismal anointing as a preliminary gift of the Spirit.

Fr Boris explains: " 'for no one can say, "Jesus is Lord," except by the Holy Spirit' (I Cor 12:3). Consequently, the preliminary descent of the Holy Spirit in our life and in the fulfillment of the sacraments is no less important than the superabundance of the Spirit given by Christ who is present in us. This discovery has been fundamental for a deepening of my theological awareness and my understanding of the meaning of the action of the Holy Spirit in the life of the Church. Indeed, the Holy Spirit is not only the One who 'comes from' and who gives us his fullness in the Church; He is also the One who introduces us, prepares us, awakens us and enables us to face baptismal combat, death and resurrection in Christ. The Holy Spirit as Awakener, as the One without whom no vocation, no recognition, no discovery of Christ can occur: there we have an idea of the preliminary maturation by the Holy Spirit, in a profound convergence between the order of 'natural creation' and the order of spiritual begetting. In both orders, the Spirit prepares the creature to receive the Word of life which places it and maintains it in the true life."

It is hard not to establish a connection between the subject of this thesis and the theologian that Fr Boris became, well known through his works on the Trinity. He himself recognizes this. "It is true that I have become attentive and sensitive very early on to the mystery and the theology of the Holy Spirit. This has been an inner, implicit reality that has deepened itself, which became more precise and crystallized more and more during the course of my life. To the degree that I became attuned to theology, the meaning and the action of the Holy Spirit became predominant, essential."

He wrote his master's thesis under the direction of Fr Georges Florovsky, who had stayed in Greece during the war and returned in 1947 to teach moral theology at St Sergius. "This is someone to whom I owe much, above all because of his stimulating view on neopatristics, and his view of the Church as the Body of Christ, a Christ-centered ecclesiology which has marked the COE very much."

Sojourn in Greece

Fr Florovsky organized for Fr Boris a two-year stay in Athens—as a student of the third cycle, invited by the Greek Church and supported financially by the COE. "I arrived in Greece in the fall of 1949. It was indeed the end of the civil war, after the victory of the regular army over the communist resistance that still controlled a part of the mountain villages, and who had taken away several thousand children and had brought them to Bulgaria to give them an ideological formation. An absolutely tragic situation! I settled in the house of the theology students in Athens. I certainly knew classical Greek from my secondary studies and from St Sergius, but I did not understand one word of the language of the country. However, in a strange manner, I have learned the language almost effortlessly. Greek 'entered into me' through some type of inner movement, of an unconscious or subconscious mechanism to such a degree that even today, after being away for almost fifty years, I continue to speak it fluently, spontaneously."

In Athens, he took courses of particular interest to him: dogmatic and liturgical theology and paleography. Above all, he developed personal bonds with some professors. He also traveled in the rest of the country—Meteora, where he visited the monasteries, and in the islands, notably at Paros, in the monastery of Longovarda, where he shared a cell with Fr Cyril Argenti,[3] who had just been ordained a priest. At Mount Athos, he passed the three months of summer, crossed the entire island starting from the Russian monastery of St Panteleimon, and studied the Palamite manuscripts, which he itemized—an activity that would serve both him and Fr John Meyendorff in his research on St Gregory Palamas. He was so taken by his sojourn on the Holy Mountain that he returned with a friend the next year at Easter, this time visiting the hermits in the desert of Karoulia, notably Fr Nikon Strandman, a friend of the Russian imperial family, who received him.

In June 1951, he had the privilege of participating in a pilgrimage by boat in honor of the nineteen-hundredth anniversary of the voyages of St Paul in Greece. On this occasion, the Greek Church, the university, and the state chartered a steamship and invited numerous personalities from the entire world, among them Msgr Cassien, Fr Georges Florovsky, and Leon Zander. As a young student fluent in several languages, Fr Boris worked in the Department of Order and Reception. "We crossed the Aegean Sea, Rhodes, Cyprus, Crete, Thessaloniki, Philippi, and Corinth. A truly remarkable trip, which ended in an apotheosis on the Areopagus in Athens and with a celebration in the Cathedral of St Paul."

Following this, he took part in an ecumenical voyage of inspection on an airplane chartered by the COE, visiting places afflicted by the war in Greece and Yugoslavia. He finally returned to France in July 1951.

What did he remember from his sojourn in Greece? Above all, the discovery of another facet of Orthodoxy: "At St Sergius, I knew only that, for me, the *Typikon*[4] and the liturgical tradition, as they were

---

[3]A priest at Marseille, Fr Cyrille Argenti (1914–1994) was one of the great figures of Orthodoxy in Western Europe.

[4]The collection of rules that govern the liturgical and ascetic life of the Church.

lived at the institute, represented the *nec plus ultra* of the unchanging truth of Orthodoxy. Suddenly I was in Greece, in different places, and I became aware of the existence of other traditions which I did not always know, which I could perhaps criticize, but which ultimately had their value and their reason for being. This has given me a type of multiple, in-depth vision, of the liturgical life of Orthodoxy. I understood then that one should not enclose oneself in one's own vision, but that we should learn how to know and love, and take seriously the different traditions that exist. In this sense, this sojourn has been very educational for me."

Marriage and Priesthood

Upon his return from Greece, the St Sergius Institute, still suffering from the departure of fathers Georges Florovsky and Alexander Schmemann for the St Vladimir Institute in New York, invited Fr Boris to take charge of the students and to teach the history of the ancient East. Two years later, at the beginning of 1954, he was offered the chair of dogmatic theology, which had been vacated with the departure of Sergius Verhovskoy, who had succeeded Fr Sergius Bulgakov and Alexis Kniazeff. He accepted this position with joy and still retains the position today. His first course dealt with the Holy Trinity.

In January 1957, he married Hélène Disterlo; three children were born from this union. Before embarking upon this road, had he been "tempted" by monasticism? "I did consider it; who does not think about it? The idea had crossed my mind very early, when I was a student at St Sergius. I happened to go then to a small monastery in Champagne. I had been asked during my stay on Mt Athos, as well as in Athens where the priest of the Russian parish who had asked me to preach on Sunday was looking for someone to replace him. I remember that I wrote to my spiritual father to ask for his advice. He replied to me: 'If you want to drink the chalice to the last drop, you can stay: But I suggest that you first return to Paris, and that you think about it to discern if it is really the will of God. You can always return to Greece afterwards.' I obeyed him: and indeed I did not return to

Athens. I examined myself and finally I sensed that it was not really my vocation."

In the Orthodox Church, marriage does not prevent access to the priesthood and therefore was not an obstacle to Fr Boris's childhood dream. Thus in 1959, he was ordained deacon in the spring and priest in the fall. "Priesthood comes in its time, as an inward evidence. The concrete and practical implications of this undertaking cannot be known and are not foreseeable. The mark of the Spirit is unconditional and the grace of the priesthood always signifies an 'objective' conformation to Christ, the Spirit-bearer, no longer for our personal sanctification but for the harvest of the Lord. Our sanctification lies in our effort to obey, and in daily purification, in a feeling of a powerful contradiction between the power of God acting through us and our own weakness and unworthiness. That married people can be called to the priesthood always remains one of the certainties of the early Christian tradition that Orthodoxy has kept lovingly, thereby witnessing through a living experience to the profound compatibility between the priesthood and married life. Certainly, every married priest knows the tensions and the rifts evoked by St Paul (I Cor 7:32–35). But marriage and human fatherhood certainly assure an affective and spiritual stability, open the heart and mind to the most complex and painful human needs and situations, and—perhaps paradoxically—ensure a real inner availability for the service of God and neighbor."[5]

Ecumenical Undertaking

Fr Boris's lack of parish responsibility at St Sergius allowed him to contribute to the ecumenical movement, which he viewed as a "permanent dimension" of his priesthood. Upon his arrival at St Sergius in the wake of Professor Leon Zander, he participated, from 1946 to 1949, in several meetings of young people and students in Europe at Oslo, Lund, and Amsterdam. He also made several trips to England

[5]"Expérience pastorale dans l'Eglise orthodoxe d'aujourd'hui," *Unité des chrétiens*, no. 58, (April 1985) 19.

under the auspices of the Fellowship of St Alban and St Sergius. In the early 1960s, he served on several theological committees of "Faith and Constitution" within the framework of the World Council of Churches (WCC), notably the one that focused on liturgy—an activity which he considered to be "decisive for the future" for two reasons. First, it gave him a chance to carry out one of his first theological studies, entitled *Ascension et liturgie.*[6] Second, he struck a close, personal friendship with the Swiss pastor Jean-Jacques von Allmen, with whom he shared the same theological and liturgical vision of the eucharistic renewal. As a result of this brotherly relationship, the former invited him to come to the theological faculty at Neuchâtel, as one in charge of doctoral candidates and of research.

Thus in 1965, Fr Boris and his family—already enriched by two children—disembarked at Neuchâtel, thanks to a grant from the national Swiss Research Fund and the WCC. The Bobrinskoys moved into the presbytery of Fenin in Val-de-Ruz. "The Reformed Church of the canton of Neuchâtel had put at our disposal a large, three-story house with ten rooms, an enormous garden, on the very slope of the mountain of Chaumont. We spent two splendid years over there, very sweet, during which we were able to grow stronger, physically and morally. My wife taught mathematics at Cernier. I was enrolled in the doctoral program of the faculty of theology with 'The Trinitarian Structures of the Sacrament of the Eucharist in the Fourth Century' as subject of the dissertation. I had chosen Jean-Louis Leuba as my dissertation director; I was taking his courses as well as those of von Allmen, Rordorf, and Menoud. We also created links with the community of sisters at Grandchamp, where I celebrated the Liturgy regularly. This stay represented for me a true theological rejuvenating experience; I received there a surge of productivity, of creativity, of extraordinary vital energy of which I benefited for several years, in a totally unexplainable manner."

In 1967 the Bobrinskoy family returned to France. Fr Boris resumed his teaching at St Sergius and continued working in the

---

[6]This text is found in Boris Bobrinskoy, *Communion du Saint Esprit*, Abbeye de Bellefontaine, coll. "spiritualité orientale" (no. 56) 71–91.

ecumenical movement. When, the following year, in the wake of Vatican II, the Higher Institute for Ecumenical Studies was created in Paris within the framework of the Institut Catholique, he became the Orthodox official in charge, at the side of Fr Le Guillou. Of this ecumenical undertaking, he later said, "I consider it a blessing of God that I was able to participate in the ecumenical dialogue and that I was constantly pushed to give an explanation of my faith to my non-Orthodox brethren in a spirit of fidelity and loyalty to the Orthodox tradition, but also of discretion and respect, faithful to the impulses of the Spirit in our divided Christendom."[7]

Parish Priest

In 1969 a tragic event occurred that would change Fr Boris's course in life. Fr Pierre Struve, priest of the French-speaking parish of the Holy Trinity of the Russian Archdiocese of the Ecumenical Patriarchate, died in a brutal accident. "Almost from one day to the next, I was in charge of this small parish which had been in existence for three or four years, and which celebrated in French in the crypt of the cathedral in Daru Street. It was a very small family which had gradually developed to become a true community." Today it remains, numerically, the most important French-speaking parish in Paris.

No matter how ready Fr Boris felt inwardly, the implications of this new charge were not evident at once: "Thrown into the Lord's field, I had the distinct feeling that my entire apprenticeship had been reduced to nothing, that everything remained to be rediscovered: the liturgical celebrations, confessions, spiritual direction, preaching."[8] As he describes it, being the pastor of a community meant that "the demands and needs of people acquired rapidly a quasi-absolute priority over the other domains of our life: the family, teaching, research. Tensions are produced, and the choices are difficult."[9]

[7]"Expérience pastorale dans l'Eglise orthodoxe d'aujourd'hui," 20.
[8]Ibid.
[9]Ibid.

In his new duties, Fr Boris experienced "the rift between the Orthodox circles of Russian language and tradition and the growing demands of groups and people of French expression." The services at the French-speaking parish—a crossroad of languages and cultures— a place of welcome for the Lebanese, the Romanians, the Russians, and the French, constituted from the outset "an incomparable spiritual enrichment which did elevate it to the horizon of a universal Orthodoxy." Still, Fr Boris has always remained faithful to his cultural and spiritual roots, and he is attached to the spiritual tradition of the Russian Church which gave him birth: "Until the end of my life, the Russian language (and Slavonic) will remain the languages of my intimate prayer, the languages in which, since my childhood, I have memorized hymns and liturgical prayers."[10]

This two-fold dimension of being rooted in a specific tradition and of openness to other traditions made Fr Boris a key player in inter-Orthodox dialogue. In his activities within St Sergius Institute—the influence of which largely transcended the boundaries of the Russian Archdiocese of the Patriarchate of Constantinople—and in his work in the Orthodox Fraternity in Western Europe, he ceaselessly worked toward the in-gathering of Orthodox of all origins, toward the emergence of a local church, beyond juridical and ethnic boundaries. In particular, he inspired and supported the creation of an inter-episcopal committee, which became the Assembly of Orthodox Bishops of France.

Henceforth Fr Boris's life unfolded between these two poles: Holy Trinity parish and his teaching at St Sergius Institute, of which he became dean in 1993, after the resignation of Professor Constantin Andronikov, who had succeeded Fr Alexis Kniazeff. This would affect the intensity of his concrete commitment to the ecumenical movement. His last important contribution was in 1978, his participation in a theological committee on the *filioque*.[11] On this fundamental question—a stumbling block in the Roman Catholic and Orthodox

---

[10]Ibid.

[11]The doctrine according to which the Holy Spirit proceeds from the Father *and* the Son, unlike what the Creed of Nicaea-Constantinople (381) states, according to which the Holy Spirit proceeds solely from the Father.

dialogue—he tried to develop an approach that would allow for a moving beyond the traditional impasses.

For a person like Fr Boris, who has known the great hope of the post-war "Glorious Thirties of Ecumenism" and who has been one of the workers at this large "theological building site," the actual weakening of the ecumenical movement—of which the crisis of WCC is but one of the symptoms—and the withdrawal from the WCC and the hardening of the Orthodox Church since the fall of the Berlin wall in 1989 are a source of suffering. "There is a great crisis of conscience with respect to ecumenism, which makes the space for action more and more limited and difficult. In several countries, the noteworthy and encouraging ecclesial renewal is accompanied by a religious and confessional contraction in various circles, monastic or other, within the parameters of an Orthodoxy in search of its identity and which often knows nothing except that it is "against": against the other churches, the Catholics, the Protestants, and the Uniates. In fact, the situation is extremely complex. An enormous gulf exists between what is experienced in certain Orthodox countries where—it must be said—there reigns a great ignorance on the reality of ecumenism, and what is lived in countries like France where real desires and possibilities exist for listening, for understanding, and for common prayer. Where is all this going to end? I could not tell. The future is truly uncertain."

One thing is certain: There will be no progress in ecumenism without a respect for the other and an inward, permanent conversion. "The Orthodox Church can only appeal to unity and for a return of the separated churches only if it searches beforehand to authenticate and actualize its own collegial, eucharistic, and sacramental life as well as its organization because it is threatened by grave dangers: dogmatic hardening, ritualism, conservatism, intolerance towards communities that are outside, and aestheticism. Consequently, the primacy of love expresses infinite respect for the other and therefore passes through a shared repentance for the weight of the past."[12]

[12]*Sainteté et unité de l'Eglise*, 28th General Assembly of the National Catholic Commission for Ecumenism (November 26, 1994).

Personality and Charisms

When evoking the various moments of his biography, Fr Boris often significantly stated: "There we have the seeds of . . ." For a disciple of the church fathers, this expression causes no surprise. Life in Christ is an actualization of the "seeds" of grace freely given in baptism (Cyril of Jerusalem), of the "passing" from the spiritual state of a child to that of an adult (Irenaeus of Lyons), and of "*epectasis*" (Gregory of Nyssa)—that is, an infinite ascending movement toward God, "from beginning to beginning, by beginnings which have no end." The entire life of Fr Boris emerges, then, as the discovery, the maturing, the developing of "charisms" that expressed themselves mainly in four domains: the liturgical service, preaching, spiritual fatherhood, and theological research and teaching.

The Liturgical Service

As a parish priest, Fr Boris was the initiator of liturgical reform—not of "experiences," with the element of adventure that word may convey. "When I took over for Fr Pierre Struve, I understood immediately—I sensed—that I had to proceed with certain innovations. I made these with moderation—step by step, being aware of limits that are not to be overstepped—mainly in five areas: the opening of the royal doors during celebration; the reading aloud of the 'secret' prayers, because the eucharistic prayer is of concern to all the faithful (the *epiclesis* crowns the memorial, and the *anamnesis* is a prayer of the entire people of God who concelebrate); the celebration of the pre-sanctified [Liturgy] in the evening; the integration of baptism into the Liturgy; and the rediscovery of the proper status of confession, which must not be reduced to a more or less obligatory preamble to Communion. Very spontaneously, organically, a liturgical vision imposed itself with some sort of 'co-naturality' with what was done in America under the influence of fathers Alexander Schmemann and John Meyendorff."

Indeed, Fr Boris became more and more sensitive to the new problems caused by the implanting of Orthodoxy in the West: "The

translation of liturgical texts into local languages invariably raises the
problem of a simplification of certain turns of phrase and liturgical
formulas in order to avoid, for example, redundancies and Byzantine
repetitions. We also feel the need for a greater transparency, openness,
communication between the celebrant and the people without—and
this is where danger lurks—compromising the sacred and mysterious
character of worship which the iconostasis preserves."[13] Unlike what
some may think, it is not a matter "of modernizing fads of certain
crypto-Orthodox parishes, but of a growing consensus in large
regions of Orthodoxy in the West. At the close of this century, in a
world that is deeply secularized and 'de-sacralized,' the liturgical life is
called to take on its missionary, catechetical dimension. More than
ever it becomes a pedagogy of the faith, of the life in God, of the mystery of ecclesial communion."[14]

Preaching

As a priest, Fr Boris cannot imagine not preaching. He likes to quote
St Paul: "Woe to me if I do not preach!" (1 Cor 9:16). He is impelled
by an inner necessity, by a deep feeling, or, better still, by a sense of
duty. "There are particularly four moments where I feel the importance of preaching, where I do not have the right to celebrate without
preaching: the celebration of the Eucharist, baptism, marriage, and
the funeral. There we must speak, encourage, console, give a meaning
to things."

For Fr Boris, "preaching is a meditation on the basis of the
Gospels, sometimes more generally of the Bible, where one tries to
bring out certain salient points for the spiritual life. It is truly a living
word drawn from the Scriptures and the entire liturgical and ecclesial
experience, a word addressed to the people of God in a relation that I
would not hesitate to describe as 'nuptial' between the pastor and his
community. Thus, a living relationship where one senses that there

---

[13]"La tradition liturgique, évolution possible et respect des décisions prises," *Le Messager
diocésain*, no. 4 (December 1995).
[14]Ibid.

are essential things to transmit. What we have to transmit is the very life of God, the experience and the living mystery of Christ. Preaching should help us in retracing the footsteps of the Lord, in living his life through the liturgical year, feast after feast, each Sunday being a new event, a living breath of the Spirit. When I am at the ambo, to preach, I am sometimes particularly moved; the words come easily, a breath passes; at other times, it is more laborious; words come with greater difficulty. But it is always a mystery: it happens that one speaks well and things pass badly or, inversely, that we speak poorly and things go better. Here we have the imponderable aspect of the living word that comes as a type of grace, and in which we sense that, ultimately, it is not we who speak but the Holy Spirit, to whom we must simply open ourselves. At the beginning, I wrote down my homilies, and I read them; then I wrote them out, I had notes, but I did not read them. Now, generally, I no longer write them. In all cases, there is always a great tension." In more than thirty years of preaching, Fr Boris has built up a considerable body of homiletics.[15]

Spiritual Fatherhood

Spiritual fatherhood imposed itself on Fr Boris gradually through the years of his priesthood. "Welcoming all the persons who come to me with their sufferings, their difficulties, their sins, their struggles; to accompany them and guide them on their way to God and with God, all this represents an important aspect of my life, which I live very deeply," he declares.

But what is spiritual fatherhood? "It is, in the vision of the fatherhood of God, helping a person to be born to life, becoming an adult, reaching the age of Christ, resembling 'the perfect man fully mature with the fullness of Christ Himself' (Eph 4:13), so that a person can finally become father and mother. It is somewhat like the work of a midwife or nurse: to help God engender sons and daughters; to partake in their birth and in the conversion of their heart. In every spiritual conversation I sense how much, with the suffering person who

[15]A collection will be edited by the Editions du Cerf, and Le sel de la terre.

has come to see me, we try to meet one another, to understand each other. Sometimes, it is true, we stumble before serious problems, but what is important is that we are there, together before the Lord. A spiritual conversation takes on meaning only if there is a privileged moment of prayer: for without such prayer which unites us through God, all the words we pronounce would only be banal, formal, external words. I try to live this spiritual fatherhood as a bond of deep mutual respect, freedom, and spiritual rigor, without imposing anything or burdening the person, but by helping him or her discern the way with all its demands."

Theological Reflection

The priestly vocation of Fr Boris began in early childhood and remained one of the constants of his life. However, his studies at St Sergius awakened in him a distinct taste for theological studies: "I passed, as it were, through a baptism of the mind, which led me not merely to sense and live inwardly something of the mystery of God, of the Holy Spirit and the Eucharist, but also to attempt formulating it. Actually, all this has happened a little in spite of myself, in the sense that I was led by the demands of the moment, pushed by urgencies. Thus, I have written most often in answer to requests. In retrospect, however, I see that in one way or the other all these requests and suggestions moved in the same direction, merged in some type of main current, as in a great river."

Such working upon request, as well as necessarily taking on numerous and heavy burdens, clarify why Fr Boris, though having written and talked much, has written very few books. Indeed, what has been published until now in book form is a collection of essays[16] and one of his theology courses at the St Sergius Institute.[17] The latter clearly shows the link between Fr Boris's reflective life and his

---

[16]*Communion du Saint Esprit.*

[17]*Le Mystère de la Trinité. Cours de théologie orthodoxe,* edit. du Cerf (1986) 331. [English translation by Anthony P. Gythiel, *The Mystery of the Trinity. Trinitarian Experience and Vision in the Biblical and Patristic Tradition,* St Vladimir's Seminary Press (1999)].

teaching—his work as a professor nourishes him as much as he nourishes it. "To be frank, I am not a teacher at all," he admits. "Through my teaching, which has been shaped, modulated, crystallized over forty years, I have tried to transmit a certain number of basic things such as the living mystery of the Trinity, the richness of the activity of the Holy Spirit in the life of the Church."

Liturgist, preacher, spiritual father, theologian, professor: all these activities of Fr Boris—the many facets and charisms of his personality—complete, interpenetrate, and nourish one another. The same inner dynamic, where life and thought are one, inspires them. "One of the distinctive aspects of my life is the connection, the studied, deeply felt unity between the priestly ministry and theological knowledge. Whatever the quality of my theological teaching, it has represented for me an invaluable enrichment, enlightening my ministry, inspiring and structuring my preaching, giving a greater consistency to my entire pastoral activity."[18]

Spirituality and Engagement in the World

This unity—of life and thought, of spirituality defined as the life of Christ in the Spirit, and of theology as a reflection on the mystery of God—is one of the keys to the testimony of Fr Boris. Expressed particularly well in several texts of *The Compassion of the Father*, it runs across his entire life and is irrigated by three springs: the liturgical tradition and the "right praise" of God, the *philocalic* tradition of purification of the heart, and the biblical and theological tradition of the church fathers.

The Unity of Theology and of the Spiritual Life

The human being, on a quest for union with the Holy Trinity and for inner unity between the heart and the mind, cannot dissociate the Eucharist, prayer, asceticism, and mental labor. Purification of the

---

[18]"Expérience pastorale dans l'eglise orthodoxe aujourd'hui," 20.

mind and thoughts, through the invocation of the Name of Jesus Christ and the sacramental life, are indispensable in approaching and describing the mystery—by essence inaccessible and unfathomable—of Christ and the Trinity. Purification prevents the reduction of this mystery to a mere theological doctrine or a scholastic speculation, to its enclosure in a language that inevitably is inadequate, because it is human.

The concern to keep together—while distinguishing between them—the theological-dogmatic awareness and the spiritual life has led Fr Boris to refute vigorously the "jest" of Patriarch Athenagoras who declared, in the glorious days of ecumenism: "We will put all the theologians on an island, and while they discuss theology, we will love one another and we will create unity."

For Fr Boris, this proposition expressed "the experience of a painful distortion between the true life of the Church and academic theology" for several reasons. First, the patristic understanding of theology is never a discourse *on* God on the basis of a purely intellectual reflection but a knowledge *of* God based on an experience of communion, of co-knowledge with God: "Christianity is not merely a doctrine. I would say it is, above all, a living experience of the Church, an experiencing of God, a communion with God, a divine life that communicates itself, that is poured out, and wells up in abundant waves, which reaches us and penetrates us in our deepest being, which overwhelms us sometimes, which questions us unceasingly because it requests our freedom and our love."[19]

Second, the patriarch's proposition distorted the relationship between love and truth: "The Orthodox faith—the word is understood here in its doctrinal and not confessional sense—is defined by the awareness that we depend upon divine truth which is revealed to us, which we attain progressively and by which we try to live in the deepest way possible. This truth is alive. It is the truth of God, a personal truth—hypostatic to use theological language—the truth of the Divine Persons, particularly of Christ who says about Himself: 'I am the Way, the Truth, and the Life" (Jn 14:6). When we speak of the truth,

---

[19]Homily for the Sunday of the Triumph of Orthodoxy (March 8, 1987).

of the truth of the Orthodox faith, we should recall that in God—and consequently in the depth of our being—truth and life are but one, truth and love are but one, truth and holiness are but one, and, lastly, truth and beauty are but one. Beauty is one of the most important aspects of the divine glory that sets the world ablaze. We discover it in each flower, in each herb, in every living being—animal or man. For God is at the same time one and three. The Trinity is one divinity and at the same time the infinite fullness of life, of the gift and of energy. In God all is one, in God all is fullness."[20]

Having said this, Fr Boris is well aware of the real danger of an academic approach to theology, notably of the divorce that can exist between, on the one hand, the teaching and initiation into theology and, on the other, the life of prayer and the living service of the Church in all its forms. "The risk is always there of enclosing oneself in a school-type theology, scholastic and speculative. Nonetheless, one of the great qualities of Orthodoxy in the West in comparison with countries of Orthodox tradition is, it seems to me, that it has been able to develop and show a vivid awareness of such pitfalls. Through the teaching of 'masters' such as Fr Alexander Schmemann and Fr John Meyendorff, or bishops Anthony Bloom, Georges Khodr, and Kallistos Ware; in circles such as the Orthodox Fraternity in Western Europe or the Syndesmos movement in full renewal; through publications such as *Contacts* and *Service Orthodoxe de Presse*; or by associations like the Christian Action of Russian Students or the one surrounding St Silouan—a living milieu that demands knowledge, possesses an amazing theological awareness, and engages in the Church and the city has been created. In this sense, the contribution of the Orthodox West is rather unique and important for the entire Church."

The Unity of the Sacred and the Profane

The word "engagement," another concern of Fr Boris, appears notably in his editorials of *Bulletin de la Crypte*,[21] where he takes a position on

---

[20]Ibid. (March 3, 1997).
[21]Monthly bulletin of information of the Orthodox parish of the Holy Trinity, in Paris.

subjects of realism. In these editorials, he refuses to separate the spiritual life and the ordinary life, the profane and the sacred, because he sees in this separation one of the sources of the "anxiety of evil of today." Contrary to the ambiguous concept of the "spiritual life": "There is, in the ultimate reality of things, no nonspiritual life, that is, a domain that is closed to the Holy Spirit. Nothing can subsist, either in the creaturely world or in the angelic world, without this hope and this binding and loving breath of the Spirit. The world that is called profane is in reality a profaned world. And man is responsible for this profanation. We have expelled God from this world; we do it every day. We chase him from the public life by a Machiavellian form of separation between our private lives—pious and good—and the domains of politics, commerce, science, technology, love, culture, and work, where everything is allowed. All these domains of human activity depend upon the creative work of man, seized, modeled, and inspired by the Spirit of God. Even when he is unaware of it, man is created in the image of God, of the Son of God who has received the command to inhabit and cultivate the world and to make of it a fertile garden. What has become of this garden? God does not accept being relegated to a well-closed recess, closed to the periphery of being. Consequently, the spiritual life signifies a quality of life according to the Holy Spirit, a polarization of all of life and of the entire human being turned toward God and in God, toward the other."[22]

The Sacrament of the Poor

This profound unity manifests itself in "the liturgy beyond the Liturgy," which St John Chrysostom called "the sacrament of the poor or of the brother," stating, "How can one celebrate the Eucharist on the altar, with precious ornaments and golden chalices, and neglect the Body of Christ at the church door: the poor one?" [*Hom 50,3* on the Gospel of Matthew; *Hom 20,3* on 2 Corinthians]. Fr Boris is very sensitive to this question. He is very pleased to see how "in the wake

[22]"Le mystère du Christ, fondement de notre prière et de notre vie," *Contacts*, no. 125 (1984) 71–122

of Mother Maria Skobtsova[23] voices that are more and more numerous are being raised to recall the urgency of brotherly love and of the diaconal dimension of the Eucharist itself."

"There is a 'before' of worship and an 'after.' The 'before' is the preparation, the march to the altar which implies an asceticism of preparation, of repentance, of work, of self-forgetfulness, of fasting, of expectation, of a growing love of Christ, which is inscribed in the week. The 'after' is the return to the world when, after partaking of the Eucharist, we are filled with the true light which we have 'seen'; we have become vessels of the Holy Spirit, of his joy and his peace which we have to preserve and shine forth in our home, our work, our life in the world."[24]

He reminds us that the dismissal of the faithful at the end of the Liturgy does not signify their "departure from the church, but their entry into the world by the preaching of the gospel, for a living testimony to Christ."[25] The preeminent means of maturation and union between this "before" and this "after" is the prayer of the heart, a true "inward liturgy" of thanks and of laying down beings and things before the name of the Lord. "We offer him, from moment to moment, our entire life and that of the world."

Fr Boris made this "diaconical" engagement, this joining of action to the word, concrete by his active participation in the Christian Association for the Abolition of Torture (in French, *ACAT*) and in the launching of the *Voix de l'Orthodoxie*. "In 1978, I was asked to help create a broadcasting center of religious, catechetical, liturgical, and theological programs. That was done rapidly, with the help of various faculties of theology, of several personalities of the Orthodox and Catholic world, of the German and Swiss Lutheran churches or of an institute such as *Glaube in der 2.Welt*. And thus, we were able to broadcast regularly on short wave two or three hours per week.

---

[23]Mother Marie Skobtsova (1891–1945) lived her monasticism in the world at the service of all those wounded by life and those who were excluded. She was deported to Ravensbrück for having saved Jews. See *Le Sacrement du* frère, Le sel de la terre (1995) 199. [For a biography of Mother Maria, see Fr Sergei Hackel, *Pearl of Great Price*, St Vladimir's Seminary Press (1981)].

[24]"L'eucharistie, rencontre de l'human et du divin," *Le Messager orthodoxe*, no. 116 (January 6, 1991) 56.

[25]"La liturgie, communication de l'Evangile," *Communion et Communication* (1978) 75–80.

Initially the broadcasting was done from Portugal. The radio reached its peak in 1988, on the occasion of the millennium of the baptism of Russia. These broadcasts continue even today. We are now trying to install ourselves in Russia itself, where we already have contacts in St Petersburg. Even ten years after the end of communism, these broadcasts remain useful and important, given the present economic and religious crisis which is rampant in Russia."

Such *diakonia* (service) and concern for the poor "behind whose face emerges the face of the One who made Himself poor in a limitless love"[26]—is still not developed sufficiently in Orthodox communities. For twenty years Fr Boris has asked forcefully and prophetically in editorials, whether, faced by "the decay of the world," the Orthodox are not inclined toward a certain "indifference, beyond momentary enthusiasms and spectacular gestures, perhaps because of the spiritual comfort of the liturgical worship, its beauty and its grace."[27]

"It is true that the Orthodox communities, sometimes foreign in relation to the social life of the country, lacking coherence and means, are themselves occupied with their own survival. But this survival in the transmission of the Orthodox faith, can it be done today outside a climate of love and compassion, without which all our preaching, all our liturgical splendor would turn out to be sad fronts hiding our own nakedness and our lukewarm attitude? Christ Himself knocks at the door of our hearts like one begging for love, under the face of the homeless, the unemployed, all those who are hungry and thirsty for love and bread. Will we be able to recognize him, to receive him, clothe him, feed him, love him? . . . [28] Where is Orthodoxy and where are the Orthodox in this difficult awakening of solidarity? More than the sending of money or food, we should acquire a new mentality, on a collective scale. It is no longer possible to isolate ourselves in our national and local 'particularisms.' Humanity is an organic body all the members of which are united by living bonds. 'If one part suffers, every part suffers with it'(1 Cor 12:26), says St Paul. For spiritual

---

[26]*Bulletin de la Crypte*, no. 129 (January 1985).
[27]Ibid. (October 1980).
[28]Ibid., no. 239 (January 1996).

solidarity finds its foundation in the infinite compassion of the Savior who gathers in Himself the entire human family."[29]

Theological Vision

Fundamentally a man of tradition, Fr Boris engendered specific, personal, new contributions among the numerous facets of his theological reflection and spiritual vision. Beyond or even within his treatment of classical themes, the two, coupled movements that animate his vision and his word are striking: light-darkness, descent-ascent. A double dynamism—paradoxical and antinomian—appear notably in the privileged place of the living Word, his preaching.

The Vision of God as Goal of the Christian Life

For Fr Boris, the theme of a vision of God is central: it fully explains the goal of the Christian life. "The living human being is the glory of God; and human life is the *vision* of God,"[30] said St Irenaeus of Lyons. Job, whom Fr Boris likes to quote, cried out from the depth of his suffering, "I know that my redeemer lives, and that in my flesh I will *see* God" (Job 19:25b). At the end of each eucharistic liturgy, the people of God say, "We *have seen* the true Light." Likewise, icons are "the breaking in of the glory and the beauty of the eternal Kingdom."[31]

This vision cannot be dissociated from this "renting of the heavens" and this "descent of God to earth" already foreseen by Isaiah (63:19), actualized by the Incarnation and made manifest notably at the time of the Baptism and the Transfiguration of Christ. "Truly, truly, I tell you, you shall see heaven open and the angels of God ascending and descending on the Son of Man" (Jn 1:51), Jesus tells Nathaniel.

---

[29]Ibid. no. 200 (February 1992).
[30]Irenaeus of Lyons, *Contre les hérésies*, IV, 20, 7, ed. du Cerf (1985) 474.
[31]"Prèface" to Michel Quenot, *L'Icône*, ed. du Cerf (1987) 7.

"To see heaven open": For Fr Boris, these four words signify the very mystery of Christ, of the Christian faith and hope. "For we have the certainty that heaven, which opened three times in the unfolding of the mystery of salvation, remains henceforth open forever. Nothing and no one can reconstruct the barrier that the sin of the first man erected between God and man. No one can excavate again the abyss which Jesus has filled between heaven and earth."[32]

While upholding this conviction, Fr Boris, nevertheless, asks this question: "If the heavens are truly open, for a moment, at the time of the birth of Christ at Bethlehem, at his ascension and at the descent of the heavenly fire at Pentecost, can they no longer be closed?" To this thought-provoking question, Fr Boris replies: "The opening of the heavens by Christ is fundamental and irrevocable because it is of an ontological order; through it, we are already in the mystery of the Trinity and in the Church. However, who of us can boast about the vision of God? As for the apostles, it can only be provisional because our eyes are still covered with scales, darkened by our passions. 'The light shines in the darkness and the darkness did not overtake it,' St John said" (Jn 1:5).

In the antinomian thought of Fr Boris, the meaning of the darkness is twofold: as a "negative" symbol of evil, temptation and death, and as a "positive" symbol of sleep, of surrender, of being buried in the earth, of the deeper meeting with the Lord who is there and who loved going away to pray during the night. "When I speak of darkness, I often think of Christ carried in the tomb and descending to Hades, and of these Gospel words: 'Except a corn of wheat fall in the ground and die, it abides alone, but if it die, it brings forth much fruit' (Jn 12:24). This is a deep spiritual reality that appears very well in icons, particularly those of the Nativity and of the Resurrection: before being illumined, the darkness must become the place of germination of the Light, in silence, in expectation, like some type of secret becoming. Our entire being, all our intelligence, must penetrate into the inner darkness to meet Christ and be changed there; must carry out the turning of conversion, the baptismal rebirth, and reemerge thus

[32]Homily for the Sunday of the Triumph of Orthodoxy (March 19, 1989).

into the Light. The entire old man must die, must surrender to the Lord, in order to be reborn and live again. No being can reach the Light without passing through such darkness."

The Cross and the Ascension

The Cross is the obligatory passage through death and darkness, which no true disciple of Christ can avoid. "A new tree of life on which we, following the example of the Son of Man, are *elevated*, according to an ascending movement which contradicts the law of earthly gravitation and which constitutes the very law of the spiritual life." St Gregory of Nyssa describes this mystery of *epectasis*, of this ascent of the soul to the divine Light "from beginning to beginning, through beginnings which have no end": a movement that finds its foundation and its end in the Ascension of Christ.

"Until the end of time, Jesus is lifted up from earth in a twofold manner: on the Cross and in His glory," Fr Boris declares. "The Crucifixion occurred at a precise moment of history; even so, we have the feeling that it lasts forever in the Church, on account of our sins which continue to make the Lord suffer. But Christ was lifted up from earth in His glory on the day of His Ascension, and since then He draws us toward Him in an unceasing, irrepressible movement. We are carried along by a new force of attraction, which does not act towards below but toward the heights. And thus our entire life is defined, constructed, constituted by the life in Christ, through the power of attraction, of transformation, of benediction of the Holy Spirit who uplifts us and makes us 'one' with Christ."[33]

Though the mystery of *kenōsis* has inspired many Christian theologians, few have looked into the theme of the Ascension so insistently as Fr Boris. "It is a reality which has impressed me deeply," he declares. "Very early, since my ordination to the deaconate on the feast of the Ascension, I have been sensitive to the mystery of the priesthood of Christ who goes before us as high priest and introduces us to

---

[33]Ibid. (March 3, 1996).

the heavenly glory. As I have tried to show in my first theological reflection,[34] financed by 'Faith and Constitution,' the mystery of the eucharistic Liturgy is not only the Incarnation of Christ here below, his *kenōsis* in the flesh of the world and of man, but his elevation in an eschatological anticipation of our heavenly becoming which is inaugurated and accomplished already in the *here and now* of the Church. This is, we must say, a dimension which is almost entirely absent from Western thought."

Light-darkness, descent-ascent: the two couplets are inseparable. "The various terms are constantly and totally interactive. The Holy Spirit descends and makes Christ descend into our hearts; embodies Him in the darkness of our existence. But, he hereby awakens us to the Light, makes us live and grow in the light which uplifts us gradually." Fr Boris defines the spiritual life as the way that leads to Christ, the thrust which carries us always higher toward our heavenly fatherland: "It is the ladder on which we ascend to the Lord, laboriously, painfully, in the impassioned élan of each day. In fact, the Lord Himself is this ladder. As the goal of the ascent, he is also its start. He holds us by the hand at every step we climb. Now, this élan that pushes us beyond ourselves, which lets us overcome our discouragement, our sadness, our tiredness, our sins, is none other than the Holy Spirit. The Holy Spirit in person is this ascending force which gives us this lightness and raises us unceasingly."[35]

The Liturgy of the Heart

The locus of this double movement, where the Cross is placed distinctly, is "the heart." "The heart is the preeminent place of combat between darkness and light, of the descent of the Spirit, of the meeting and betrothal to Christ, of death and resurrection."

Between the age of eighteen, when he discovered *The Tales of the Russian Pilgrim* in an Orthodox vacation camp during the war, and the time of theological maturity, Fr Boris not only has interiorized the

---

[34]"Ascension et Liturgie," in *Communion du Saint-Esprit*, Bellefontaine (1992) 71–91.
[35]Homily for the Sunday of the Triumph of Orthodoxy (March 11, 1984).

prayer of the heart, but he also has gained an awareness of its three basic components. First, its ecclesial dimension: "There is an amazing structural consonance between the prayer of the heart and the Eucharist; the prayer of the heart is for me a Eucharistic action, the liturgy of the heart of which Scripture speaks." Second, its pre-eminently trinitarian character: "To invoke Jesus is to invoke the Father whose Son He is and with whom He is one. And, as the Apostle says, 'No one can say Jesus is Lord, except by the Holy Spirit' (1 Cor 12:3). Inspired and instructed, we can meet the Lord; and from this encounter flows the gift of the Holy Spirit who makes us fruitful and sanctifies us." Third, its biblical character: "Very quickly, I became sensitive to the fact that the early Christians called each other 'those who at all times and in every place call on the Name of the Lord' (1 Cor 1:2); consequently, the prayer of the heart is not something new introduced at Sinai or on Athos; it belongs to the most basic and elementary realities of faith and prayer. 'Everyone who calls on the name of the Lord will be saved' (Acts 2:21), St Peter said on the day of Pentecost. The *Kyrie eleison* of our liturgical offices is nothing but a summary of the prayer of the heart. I often recall that in the litany which closes the Liturgy of the Word: 'Let us all say, from the depth of our heart, let us say,' what is most important are not the words of the deacon—these are prayer intentions—but the answer of the faithful: *Kyrie eleison*."

The Mystery of the Trinity

On the strictly theological plane, Fr Boris devoted his essential work to an examination, an elucidation of the mystery of the Trinity. During his studies at St Sergius, he already had perceived intuitively that "the entire life of the Church, its liturgical and sacramental respiration and its insertion into the world, is defined within the framework of the plurality of trinitarian relationships."[36] Thus, his perspective is not speculative, but existential. For him, to speak of the trinitarian

---

[36]"Les chemins de la révélation trinitaire," *Supplément au SOP*, no. 156 (March 1991) 9.

communion is to speak of the work of God in our life—"My Father is always at work to this very day; and I, too, am working" (Jn 5:17)—of the Spirit ceaselessly at work in us to make us more and more similar to Christ. To speak of the Trinity is also to speak of the paschal mystery which reveals to us the infinite love of the Trinity, the limitless mercy of the Father "who so loved the world that He gave his one and only Son that whoever believes in Him shall not perish but have everlasting life" (Jn 3:16).

The heart of the Christian life consists of "the concrete, living discovery, at the same time personal and ecclesial, of the mystery of the Trinity; we should enter into it with the Holy Spirit Himself who turns us away from our earthly gravity and introduces us into the heart of Christ, and through Him into the heart of the Father. All this requires of us an effort, necessitates a long apprenticeship with a spiritual father, just as the acquisition of the art of the icon implies a long apprenticeship with a master. In this manner, we ourselves become images of Christ; we become a temple and a dwelling place of the Holy Trinity. The light of Christ shines in us. The words of Christ can then be fulfilled in our lives; 'Let your light shine before men, that they may see your good deeds—not your merits, but the good deeds which are the work of the Spirit and praise your Father in heaven'" (Mt 5:16).[37]

The Resting of the Spirit on the Son

A very important theme emerges from the meditation of Fr Boris on the mystery of the Trinity: the repose of the Holy Spirit on the Son. A biblical passage, which, according to Fr Boris, has played a key role in his entire life, is a text from the prophet Isaiah (61:12) read by Jesus in the synagogue of Nazareth: "The Spirit of the Lord is on me; therefore He has anointed me to preach the good news to the poor. He has sent me to proclaim freedom for the prisoners and recovery of sight for the blind, to release the oppressed, to proclaim the year of the Lord's favor" (Lk 4:18–19).

[37]Homily for the Sunday of the Triumph of Orthodoxy (March 4, 1990).

"The resting of the Spirit on the Son has become a vital truth for me these last twenty years, practically since that study in which I endeavored to reflect on the implications and the overcoming of the controversy of the *filioque*.[38] As John the Baptist says, 'The man on whom you see the Spirit come down and remain is . . . the Son of God' (Jn 1:33). An in-depth study of the Fathers gives us the key to this correspondence between the resting of the Spirit on Christ and the trinitarian mystery in itself. Starting from there, there is no need for a 'filioquism' to give an account of the mysterious relationship of the Spirit to the Son. The two go together. Coming from the Father, they interpenetrate one another: the Spirit is in the Son, the Son is in the Spirit. What we have is a complete reciprocal interiority, in eternity as well as in human life. In this sense, the *filioque* derives above all from a misunderstanding, from a narrowing or a type of restriction of the truth. If there certainly is a relationship of Christ imparting the Spirit, it does not exhaust the richness of the relationship between Christ and the Spirit. To limit oneself to this unilateral relationship, to this simple formulation of Christ as source of the Spirit is to impoverish the mystery. For we must not forget that Christ Himself is formed by the Spirit, is the bearer of the Spirit, is sent by the Spirit into the desert, and is acting in the Spirit. In this sense, the eternal mystery of the Holy Spirit is polyvalent: He prepares the Christ, He incarnates Him, and He carries Him as much as He is carried and given by Christ. All this is to be seen together. At that moment, the Holy Spirit can no longer be viewed merely as a gift—the word 'gift' always has an impersonal consonance—but He is also the Giver. And He is given, not only by the Father and the Son, but by Himself."

For Fr Boris, this reflection is not merely an intellectual exercise; like any well understood dogmatic formulation, it has consequences in our own lives: "This term 'repose of the Spirit on the Son' is decisive for our spiritual evolution because we are called to become Christ, in turn: 'My dear children, for whom I am again in the pain of childbirth until Christ is formed in you' (Gal 4:19). It is by the Holy Spirit that

[38]Boris Bobrinskoy, "The *Filioque* Yesterday and Today," in Lukas Vischer, *Spirit of God, Spirit of Christ* (London-WCC, Geneva: SPCK, 1981) 133–148; Boris Bobrinskoy, *The Mystery of the Trinity* (New York: St Vladimir's Seminary Press, 1999) 295–303.

Christ Himself is formed in us. It is to the extent that we become a dwelling place of the Spirit that we become Christ ourselves: 'You are christs,' St Cyril of Jerusalem says. The Spirit constitutes us, shapes us, and creates us in the image of Christ. The entire program of our deification is contained in the repose of the Spirit on Christ."

Having said this, the *filioque* controversy should not be underestimated, but made relativistic and overcome. It would not suffice, for example, for the Catholic Church to omit the *filioque* from the Nicene Creed to cut the Gordian knot of the thousand-year conflict that separates Orthodoxy from Catholicism: "The regulation of what is contentious in the *filioque* cannot be separated from what is contentious in ecclesiology, that is, the question of the Roman primacy facing Orthodox conciliarity."[39]

The Mystery of the Father

In his reflection on the Holy Trinity, Fr Boris is touched more and more, impressed, even overwhelmed, by the mystery of the Father, "the first and ultimate source of all knowledge and all life,"[40] which he senses is inscribed, buried in the mystery of Christ. It is the mystery of silence of the one who utters the Word and who transcends all words; the mystery of tenderness of the one who is infinite mercy and compassion, who never tires of receiving his prodigal son. "This mystery remains the greatest of all. Indeed, it is easier to speak of the mystery of Christ or even of the mystery of the Holy Spirit than that of the Father, so high does the Father dwell beyond all words. Certainly, the mystery of the Father is revealed only through Christ: 'The one who has seen me has seen the Father' (Jn 14:9). But can the mystery of the Father be reduced to these words? Is this a satisfactory answer? Then, what does one do with the irrepressible desire I feel more and more strongly, and which the apostle Philip expresses in the farewell discourse: 'Show us the Father' (Jn 14:8)? Then, why not simply pray to Christ? And what is the meaning of the *Our Father*? This is for me

[39]"Les chemins de la révélation trinitaire," 8–9.
[40]"Mystagogie trinitaire des sacrements," *Supplément au SOP*, no. 170 (July–August, 1992) 4.

a very difficult prayer, and it is not sufficient to recite it in a more or less mechanical fashion."

Fr Boris urgently expresses these essential, profoundly existential questions with conviction: "What is a father if not an overflowing of love? But do we feel it as such? How do we live this filial relationship to the Father? Do we really know the meaning of fatherhood—if only the purely human and earthly—without which this relationship to the father no longer makes much sense? Are we able to understand and to live the meaning and implications of the 'bowels of mercy' and of the tenderness of the Father? What effect does all this have on our awareness and our life? These are questions I ask myself, and I ask them aloud. Questions which the Holy Spirit Himself asks in us, by prompting us to become more aware of the mystery of the person of the Father. For the Father is not only a name: He is also a living person. A person with whom we should enter into a living and personal relationship, through Christ. How do we become sons and daughters, children of the light? In our personal or ecclesial experience, where is the prayer of the Spirit who sighs in us 'Abba, Father'? Let us remember what St Ignatius of Antioch wrote in his *Letter to the Romans*: 'A living water murmurs in me: come to the Father.'"

Rooted in the Scriptures

Fr Boris, following the tradition of the church fathers, anchors his theological reflection in the Scriptures, in the Gospel certainly, but also in the Old Testament: "In this, and from the time of my studies, I am very dependent upon the biblical renewal, Catholic and Anglican, for which I am very grateful. Thanks to it, I have learned how to take seriously the text itself, history, and the historical background. Certainly, typology is important: it is obvious that the Old Testament requires a Christian, christological, ecclesial, and sacramental reading. But such an interpretation must start from a living reality, while always connecting the spiritual vision to reality, to the entire history, which should be revalued and not merely reduced to the role of a misadventure, according to a dualistic vision of human existence. Before one develops the prophetic, messianic, and christological dimension of the text, one should pay the closest attention and rigor to the literal, literary, historic, and geographical context."

For Fr Boris, the Old Testament is the paradoxical place of the presence of God and of the expectation of the Spirit: "If the heavens are opened fully with Christ, they are already open in the Old Testament. There is an experience of God, an encounter with God, a 'rumination' of the name of God, a presence of God that is very strong, the *Shekinah*. A presence that is, at the same time, promise and anticipation. When the Jews repeat the Name of the Lord, the Name of Yahweh, something very profound occurs. There is in Judaism, up to our day, a mystery of the name of God which has been revealed and which the Church can accordingly absolutely not ignore or reject."

Regarding the presence but also the expectation of the Spirit, Fr Boris quotes the Book of Numbers, where Moses, disagreeing with Joshua, encourages Medad and Eldad to prophesy: "If only all of Yahweh's people were prophets!" (Num 11:24–30). As he has it, "What is still only a dream in the mind of Moses, an unreal dream, will be realized at Pentecost, in the New Church: 'I will pour out my Spirit on all people, your sons and daughters will prophesy' " (Acts 2:17).

This presence and this expectation of the Spirit in the Old Testament cannot be dissociated from another dimension Fr Boris feels distressingly: "The silences, the absence or the departure of the Spirit. When, in Ezekiel, one senses the glory of God rise above the temple and move away, one suddenly senses an extraordinary contrast with the effusion, the richness of the Holy Spirit in the New Testament, particularly in the infancy Gospels."

Purification and Transparency

Fr Boris's journey, personality, and vision bring to light a subtle dialectic between unity and diversity, entrenchment and openness. A unity of faithfulness to fundamental intuitions and obedience to the will of God co-exist with the diversity of charisms. Notably rooted in the Orthodox tradition—particularly the Russian tradition—yet possessing an openness to "the other," he transcends the tradition from within, assimilating of the riches of others and returning to what is essential. Olivier Clément correctly noted this latter movement as "a preoccupation with a renewed language inseparable from an ecclesial way of life and open simultaneously—well beyond the fears and the polemics—to the anxieties and intuitions of modernity."[41]

Solidly anchored in the tradition of the Church, anxious to respect and never to impoverish it, Fr Boris fearlessly and objectively critiques certain aspects of this tradition, in order to live and transmit it. His nontriumphalistic homilies on the occasion of the Triumph of Orthodoxy summarize this attitude in two words: purification and transparency.

Fr Boris insists on purification of the tradition, expressed by his plain language: "We should cleanse Orthodoxy to reach what is essential."[42] In the two millennia of its existence, Orthodoxy has developed an extraordinary liturgical, sacramental, spiritual, and iconographic richness. The danger of this profusion of texts, of gestures and symbols, when cultivated in selfish isolation, is "to mask the one thing necessary: the pearl of great price for which we must be able to abandon everything at any moment,"[43] thereby veiling the face of Christ. The latter, like the icon, is in no need of gilding because it carries in itself its own splendor: "When we turn toward Orthodoxy and the Church, we feel overwhelmed by the infinite richness manifested in its culture, its doctrine, and spirituality. And the more we discover the inexhaustible abundance of treasures accumulated in various countries, at different times and in various surroundings, the more we marvel, but are also overburdened.[44] This abundance of rituals and of forms assumed by doctrine, this very overabundance of the vestment over what is essential is almost too heavy to bear. We should be careful not to confound the mystery with this external vestment linked to various times and places. For the presence of Jesus is a reality that is simple, pure, and unique, which is not in need of many words. We

[41]"Preface" to *Communion du Saint Esprit.*
[42]"Le message orthodoxe pour nous aujourd'hui," *Supplément au SOP,* no. 207 (April 1996) 9.
[43]Homily for the Sunday of the Triumph of Orthodoxy (March 3, 1996).
[44]Ibid.

should move beyond words, figures, and symbols to contemplate the face of Jesus and, in Him, that of the Father. If we are not able to do this, our very richness condemns us."[45]

Besides purification, there is a necessary transparency. "Faced with the dangers and the numerous, varied assaults of the Clever One, the Orthodox churches show an occasional tendency to close in upon themselves, to define their identity against the surrounding world, against other religions, against non-Orthodox Christians in a confessional hardening which is humanly speaking understandable, but which limits the range of the gospel message."[46]

From this perspective, the transparency of which Fr Boris speaks "is first of all a refusal to build compartments and artificial screens between us and God, between us and the others. For we are always busy protecting ourselves, isolating ourselves, building walls behind which we take pleasure in some type of comfort, be it in our churches or in communities, which can become ghettos. Repeating a term from Fr Congar, I often insist on a church that is 'poor and a servant'—that is, one that is not its own end. And when I say 'church,' I also understand the one we carry within. For me, the Church must be at the same time totally transparent to the grace of God—of which it is the channel and the reflection—and totally transparent to the world—of which it is the spokesperson and the prayer-bearer before the face of God—while not being of the world. To say this differently: the Church must not compromise the descent of the grace of God in the world, nor the ascent of the sufferings of the world to God. Now, if the Church accentuates and hardens its own frontiers, it prevents this double mediation and it becomes opaque to both the grace of God and the needs of the world. It defines itself first by itself and is self-sufficient."

By enclosing itself in its particularities and in its own inner life, the Church betrays its basic mission, which is to be "as a light and a testimony to the infinite love of God for the world." "We should never forget that in front of us there is an immense world, a world that does

---

[45]Homily for the Sunday of the Triumph of Orthodoxy (March 18, 1973).
[46]Homily for the Sunday of the Triumph of Orthodoxy (March 3, 1985).

not know the secret that is in it, a world whose heart sighs without knowing for what, but which, fundamentally, seeks God. A world that would want to know Him, love Him, live in Him. We Christians have an immense responsibility toward that world. It seems to me that if we are filled with the Holy Spirit, we can no longer remain in ourselves cozily, holed up in our beautiful, great, and luminous Eucharistic communities. For, where it can, the Church must bring to the poor, the impoverished, the down-and-out, what it has received, namely the word and the love of God."[47]

The Church does not become impenetrable to grace and to the sufferings of the world only by self-sufficiency and an idolatrous attachment to forms. The Church also becomes this way through sin, a lukewarm attitude, and the lack of faith of its members: "Human sin tarnishes the face of the Church, compromises its testimony, makes its words ineffective and the reception of the gospel in human hearts difficult. It is not only the world that rejects the gospel and the Church, it is we, Christians, who carry them badly, who live them badly and who therefore compromise their transmission and their reception in human hearts. This is why we carry this responsibility, this fault, this *kenōsis* which did not have to be."[48]

Sin always is linked to resistance to the Holy Spirit: "We refuse his presence or we accept it only for a brief moment. Our worst fault is undoubtedly our lukewarm attitudes. As the Apocalypse says: 'If only you were warm or cold. But because you are lukewarm, I am about to spit you out of my mouth!' (Rev 3:16). Lukewarm attitudes amount to mediocrity."[49]

For Fr Boris, "We should therefore become aware of our lukewarm attitude in prayer, in faith, and in love. We should rediscover the meaning of inward prayer, of unceasing prayer, this breathing of the Holy Spirit in us, which Christianity conveys from generation to generation, the life and labor of the saints. It is our program; it is our call."[50]

---

[47]Homily for the Sunday of the Triumph of Orthodoxy (March 3, 1996).
[48]Homily for the Sunday of the Triumph of Orthodoxy (February 28, 1988).
[49]Homily for the Sunday of the Triumph of Orthodoxy (March 19, 1989).
[50]Ibid.

Our hearts will become, will be once more, the deep sanctuary of the presence of God, more and more transparent to the light of Christ. "The more transparent a windowpane is, the more it becomes invisible and faithfully transmits the light and the image. The more transparent the Church is and the more it keeps itself in the background before the message of the Savior and his life-giving presence, the more it opens itself to the service of God and people, becoming an icon of God for the people, and an icon of the people for God. In this manner, the Church, as a true icon, does not impose itself."[51]

If this spiritual law is true for the Church, it is evidently also true for any eucharistic community and for each believer who must work ceaselessly to free the inner icon from its impurities, its incrustations, from all the things that have been added to it and prevent it from being "transparent to its model," to make the glory, the light, and the grace of God shine forth in the world. "Thus, this purification must be personal, intimate and unique for each one of us, and at the same time collegial, common, social, and ecclesial."[52]

The Return to What Is Essential

This effort at purification and transparency has only one goal: the return to the essential. "What, then, is the essential?" Fr Boris wonders. "It is a living relationship of love with Christ. It is the discovery of the one Jesus of the gospel as He reveals Himself in various Orthodox and Christian cultures. This is why it is so important to make of the gospel our daily, diligent reading, for it is in the gospel that we commune with the Lord in a privileged and personal manner. The gospel, which is the Word of God, is the indispensable place of communion, the *locus* of the real presence of the Lord and of the entire Trinity."[53]

The church fathers, who gave themselves no rest until the faithful were led to the mystery of Christ—the Jesus of the Beatitudes, the

[51]Homily for the Sunday of the Triumph of Orthodoxy (March 3, 1985).
[52]Homily for the Sunday of the Triumph of Orthodoxy (March 17, 1997).
[53]Homily for the Sunday of the Triumph of Orthodoxy (March 3, 1996).

Suffering Servant who divested Himself of his divine glory to join man in his poverty and enrich him with his poverty—have never said anything different. Likewise, the purpose of the Church structures, canons, dogmas, councils, symbols, worship, and institutions is to serve the gospel, to serve the people and this world "which God so loved." In the antinomian thought of Fr Boris, the gospel and Church tradition are in accord: "Let us try to keep together the two poles of the mystery. On the one hand, the mystery of Jesus which is sufficient unto itself and speaks for itself. On the other, the mystery of the full-ness and of the profusion of riches accumulated by the Church in the Holy Spirit. For it is in it that we will live the gospel more fully and will have access, beyond words, to the full riches of the Father."[54] This deep unity leads to a query: "All the riches of our two-thousand-year-old tradition are summarized in the gospel revelation. This is the great question addressed to the Orthodox and by the Orthodox: between biblical revelation and the tradition of the Church that derived from it and leads to it, is there not a link so strong that it encompasses unity?"[55]

The Simplicity of the Testimony

Fr Boris owes this constant return to the gospel sources particularly to "the monk of the Eastern Church," Fr Lev Gillet. "Better than any other, he has shown to us that it is possible to be fully Orthodox with-out being imprisoned by all the cultural, aesthetic, artistic, and theo-logical riches accumulated over the centuries. Without falling into simplicities or into sectarian 'elementarism,' we can, while being nourished by these riches, return constantly to the essential things, in a plain language which is at the same time that of the gospel and that of today's men and women."

This approach to Christian witness is decisive for engagement in ecumenical dialogue or with a de-christianized world. "When we speak to others, we do not have to thrust at them the truths of

---

[54]Homily for the Sunday of the Triumph of Orthodoxy (March 18, 1973).
[55]*La Bible, lieu de rencontre entre les Eglises d'aujourd'hui, pro manuscripto* (1992).

Orthodoxy. We should speak to them of the simplest things, which are true, immediate, and fundamental: the mystery of Christ who has come to help us, love and save us. For this, there is no need to burden our language, our words, with an entire theological jargon, with all the formulations of the ecumenical councils. A long apprenticeship is needed before our language reaches the transparency of the icon and of the gaze of the saints. But this transparency of language to the gospel message, to the presence and the words of the Lord, is evidently only possible through the holiness and the purity of our own lives, a passionate love of the truth, and the humble love for our brothers."

For Fr Boris, faith in the gospel is the privileged place of encounter among brothers and sisters of other confessions. "In the presence of others, it is less important, it seems to me, to present myself as Orthodox or to pin up Orthodox specifics, than it is to speak of fundamental things which exist and which we find in the heart of every Christian and of every human being."

Would Fr Boris thus describe himself first as a Christian, before asserting himself as Orthodox? "One may venture to say this," he declares, "because Orthodoxy is a concept that has developed in history, while being a Christian is the first name which implies our dependence, our submission, our belonging to Christ, to his mystery and to his Church. The essential of Orthodoxy is the life in Christ: it is, simply, to be a Christian. Based on this, when I speak to other Christians, there is no need to recall that I am Orthodox: it is up to them to discover this, up to them to sense it from within."

But, what does it mean to be a Christian? "This word—which was used for the first time in Antioch to designate the disciples of Jesus— has become a general, trivialized designation, which has ceased to correspond to the living reality. Being a Christian meant, at the beginning, to be marked by Christ, by the anointing of Christ. St Cyril of Jerusalem said during the fourth century in his catechesis: 'We are anointed by the Holy Spirit; we have become christs.' 'Christs': the word designates the anointed, the chrismated, that is, persons who are set apart by the anointing and who, being marked and permeated by the grace of the Holy Spirit are called to become conformable to

Christ. We bear the name of Christ because we have engraved it in our heart. Through holy baptism we are set apart: we are sent into the world, but we are not of the world. We are sanctified, quenched by the blood of Christ, nourished by his own body, becoming one with Him, in such a manner that, according to the expression of St Paul, 'It is no longer I who live, but Christ who lives in me' (Gal 2:29). Being a Christian is this: being *in* Christ, and that Christ may be *in* me. Through this double *in*, through this double co-penetration, I accept the Lord in my heart and the Lord opens his own heart to accept me."[56]

Maxime Egger

---

[56]Homily for the Sunday of the Triumph of Orthodoxy (March 3, 1996).

Fr Boris Bobrinskoy

Facing Evil and Suffering

CHAPTER ONE

THE LAMB OF GOD TAKES UPON HIMSELF HUMAN SUFFERING

" Look, the Lamb of God, who takes away the sin of the world," John the Baptist says (Jn 1:29). In reality, what the Lamb takes upon his shoulders is infinitely more complex: a multi-faceted burden, which in a word may be termed "misery."

The Baptist applies to Jesus a stunning Old Testament prophecy in which the Law and the Prophets converge: the songs of the Suffering Servant (Is 42–55). From Pentecost onward, this "fifth Gospel" would shape the core, even the very letter, of Christian preaching. Without exception, the New Testament catechesis of the redemption of Christ formed around these passages. Thus, my reflections on the passion of Christ and the passions of humanity will be structured around them.[1]

When speaking of "the passions of men," there is a tendency to narrow the meaning to sufferings, anxieties, and struggles. One forgets the ascetic meaning—the degrading, alienating, and supreme constraint of sin and its totalitarian ascendancy over the entire human being. To speak of "passions," or "sufferings," necessitates outlining their evil causes and the roots of sin.

The Sin of the World

The Bible presents sin as a global state of disorder, as being removed from God, as inner derangement. Sin is infinitely more than that to

---

[1]This text resumes a conference given at a colloquy of the Association chrétienne pour l'abolition de la torture (ACAT), entitled "Passion du Christ, passions des hommes," on May 11 and 12, 1984, at Toulouse.

which our preaching has reduced it. By juxtaposing images, the fourth song of the Suffering Servant of Deutero-Isaiah enters into the mystery of sin: "Surely He took up our infirmities and carried our sorrows, . . . But He was pierced for our transgressions, He was crushed for our iniquities; for the transgressions of (His) people He was stricken, . . . He bore the sins of many" (Is 53:4ff).

The singular and plural mixed terms "He took up . . . our sorrows, our transgressions, our iniquities, the sins of many" represent both a human being and humanity—the one and the multiple Adam—united in solidarity and in a state of deep decay. A personal and collective alienation from God and self creates a state of dreamy illusion, reminiscent of a collective subconscious—an almost sacramental remembrance of primordial sin.

In particular, the Augustinian usage of the famous text—"the one in whom all of us have sinned" (Rom 5:12)—emphasizes a true *Crux interpretum*, the mystery of this mystical spiritual bond, this obscure *sobornost*[2] that chains humanity in sin and evil. This is the reign of death, the fruit and the wages of sin, which covers humanity.

As Fr Jacques Guillet wrote: "This corruption is without remedy, the enslavement is without solution, man cannot tear himself away from sin and only has to expect from the tyrant to whom he has been delivered the one remuneration he has at his disposal, death (Rom 6:34). The universal power of sin, the definitive slavery of sin. Sin reaches all people and it corrupts the entire person."[3]

Very early in the Old Testament and definitively in the New Testament, a personal, tyrannical force hostile to God stands behind enslavement to sin. Sin itself is personified, as St Irenaeus will say later, *peccatum peccans*—("sin sinning"). Jesus will unmask the father of lies, Satan, the Tempter, who seeks to scatter the children of God.

The sin that grows roots in the evil, reprobate heart (Jer 16:11–12) causes numberless misfortunes and grief. Further questions emerge: Where is the sin, and what is the punishment? How does one establish a boundary between the one and the other? What is the cause, and

---

[2]Derived from a Russian word meaning "council," *sobornost* expresses the idea of universal communion in which unity and plurality coexist.

[3] *Thèmes bibliques*, Aubier (1954) 101.

what is the consequence? Where is the misfortune, and where is the maliciousness? "The one and the other," Fr Guillet continues, "because the prophet Isaiah, upon seeing the ruins of his country, perceives the measureless distress of his people, he perceives 'the incurable wound' (Jer 10:19). This incurable wound is another image where suffering and the stain are fused together."[4] A mysterious logic (sin and the punishment inherent in it) causes catastrophes and misfortunes and operates neither by natural law or fate.

Disturbing concepts—the extrinsic punishment of a vengeful God and the notion of a penal and distributive justice—runs throughout the Old Testament and into the New Testament, extending to the doorstep of the Gospels and the parables of Jesus. The psalmist does state, "Yahweh's anger blazed out at the people, His own heritage filled him with disgust" (Ps 106:40). Jeremiah notes a malicious, pitiless judge: "It is your own wickedness that will punish you, your own apostasy that will condemn you" (Jer 2:19). Sin itself acts as a merciless tyrant with a dismal retinue of passions and lusts. "Therefore," St Paul concludes, "God gave them over to shameful lusts" (Rom 1:24–28). Lust recalls another cry of St Paul, "I was sold as a slave to sin" (Rom 7:14). Jesus Himself recounts the story of the poor Lazarus and the demise of the evil, rich man.

The merciless friends of Job consoled him with this logic: "You suffer; you are punished because you have sinned; repent before God." With all his being, Job refused to surrender to such exhortations and did not admit his guilt. He appealed to God, in the certainty of seeing the Redeemer with his eyes of flesh. God sided with him. Thus, Job approaches the threshold of a mystery to which Deutero-Isaiah and the Psalms give greater depth, the mystery of the innocent Just One. Job's refusal of unjust suffering still resonates in all human sufferings.

In our most elementary and natural awareness, suffering is nonsense, a scandal at the heart of God's creation; the humble heart revolts against it. It is an integral part of disorder, of sin, which sickens and enslaves all of humanity. Only by anticipating the mystery of redemption does it finally acquire sacramental, positive, pedagogical,

[4]Ibid. 123.

and revealing value, as a sign of the divine love, crucified and victorious. Jesus Christ Himself becomes the living key to the parable of the rich man and Lazarus. He fulfills and gives meaning to the image of the suffering, poor man in Sheol.

God Accepts the Challenge of Evil

This degradation, this corruption of the beautiful and good creation of God, challenges the loving plan of the trinitarian Council: "Let us create man in our image and likeness" (Gen 1:26). In these words, the Fathers saw a hidden mystery of the Council of the Divine Trinity: "And God saw all that He had made, and it was very good" (Gen 1:31). "And God rested on the seventh day." This rest of the Creator does not hint at an abyss of immobility and silence, but at a cosmic and angelic rejoicing which no words are sufficient to describe: "Man," Ezekiel says, "used to be a model of perfection, full of wisdom, perfect in beauty, walking in Eden, in the garden of God, in the midst of red-hot coals; all kinds of gems formed his mantle" (Ezek 28:12–14).

God, concerned for the destiny of His creatures, takes up Satan's challenge at the very moment disobedience is perpetrated. The promise of the Redeemer coincides with the first curse of the serpent—that sorrows and pains would be the lot of man and woman. Death would be their end, the punishment of sin.

Although the salvific and pedagogical character of sufferings and death itself would appear only later in Israel's religious awareness, God is not indifferent, impassable, or insensitive when faced with evil, human suffering, and degradation. Origen wrote an extraordinary text on the subject of a God who suffers *before* He becomes incarnate, a God whose bowels of mercy are destroyed, crushed, by the very sight of the creature's degradation. The suffering of a loving God compels him to leap into the abyss where man is about to perish. The book of Genesis visualizes the blood of Abel crying out to God (Gen 4:10) regarding the iniquity that gradually covers the earth.

The Bible frequently describes the feelings of God in anthropomorphic words, which are far from archaic, outdated concepts. God's bowels of mercy and compassion follow His anger, the distributive justice of the Decalogue. Scripture declares, "Can a woman forget her baby at the breast, feel no pity for the child she has borne? Even if these were to forget, I shall not forget you" (Is 49:15). "Go, my people, go to your private room, shut yourselves in. Hide yourselves a little while until the retribution has passed" (Is 26:20); "I did forsake you for a brief moment, but in great compassion I shall take you back. In a flood of anger, for a moment I hid my face from you. But in everlasting love I have taken pity on you, says Yahweh, your Redeemer" (Is 54:7–8ff).

Thus, from the first moment of disobedience, when Adam and Eve discover they are naked and flee from the gaze of their Creator, God goes to search for them: "Adam, where are you?" (Gen 3:9). This call of God resonates beyond the boundaries of the primitive Eden; it reverberates throughout the entire history of Israel and of humanity. God moves to search for the lost sheep, and when He has found it, He, full of joy, brings it back on His shoulders to the sheep pen. Upon His return, He gathers friends and neighbors for rejoicing (Lk 15:4–7). Again, we perceive echoes of the heavenly feast.

However, the search for the lost human being is long and hard. The Orthodox Church, at Matins of Holy Saturday, in the wake of St Irenaeus states: "You descended to earth to find Adam, but You did not find him on earth, O Master, and You went to search for him in Hades" (stanza 25).

He Loved Us to the End

The redemptive mystery of our salvation should be centered on the theme, at the same time biblical and patristic, of the identification of God and of the human being, between which there is a double movement of conferring and receiving love. St Athanasius, inspired by St Irenaeus of Lyons said, "God became man so that man might become God." This short, incisive formula sums up the mystery of salvation. St Paul already spoke of "the generosity that our Lord Jesus Christ had, that, although He was rich, He became poor for our sake, so that you should become rich through His poverty" (2 Cor 8:9). This great christological theme of *kenōsis*, of the voluntary humbling of the Son of God through obedience unto death, even death on the cross (Phil 2:6–9), also announces His exaltation above every name.

The troublesome concept of the humbling of God is central in the doctrine of the Bible and of the Church. Why was it necessary for God to humble Himself by sending His own Son to suffering, to disgrace, and to death? Either this disgrace is real and contradicts the power and the greatness of God, or it is the stage play wherein God remains unconcerned.

Instead of speculating about logical contradictions of this *kenōsis*, let us discern the stages of the creative work of the Divine Trinity, to follow the progress of the divine Love that humbles itself before the creature in order to uplift it to Him. The Bible offers mysterious glimpses of sacrificial love within the eternal crucible of the trinitarian life: "You were redeemed," St Peter says, "with the precious blood of Christ, a lamb without blemish or defect. He was chosen before the creation of the world" (1 Pet 1:18–19). Elsewhere, the Apocalypse names the just, who are "written down since the foundation of the world in the sacrificial lamb's book of life" (Rev 13:8). Without attempting an exegesis of these difficult texts, we are struck by their troubling convergence, their almost literal coincidence; they evoke the mystery of the eternal, sacrificial love of God.

By trying to destroy God's work, which is beautiful and good, Satan has neither the last word nor an understanding of the unfathomable wisdom of the Creator. Divine love—true love—is by nature a sacrificial oblation. Divine love therefore is always, in the very bosom of the Divine Trinity, a gift of self to the other, the beloved. Intra-trinitarian love is this blessed and infinite exchange which the icon of St Andrei Rublev, "The hospitality of Abraham," describes for us and which Fr Daniel Ange has celebrated so well in his work *L'Etreinte de Feu*.[5] Such trinitarian love also creates free beings, called to divine love.

God accepts being challenged, being limited. This is His divine *kenōsis*—prior to the advent of sin—His overabundance of love.

---

[5] *L'Etreinte de Feu, l'Icône de la Trinité de Roublev*, Desclée de Brouwer, 1980.

Kenotic sacrifice springs from divine roots. Suffering appears later, when this divine love is questioned, ridiculed, rejected. Thus, divine mercy moves in the presence of pride, of the lie, of evil upsurges that invade the earth like gangrene, like the sand of the desert invades the fertile land. As sin emerges and spreads, God is compelled by His own love—and also by His very faithfulness and justice—to "leave" His blessed infinity, to reach man in the inferno of his delinquent, distressed heart. The entire history of humanity, and therefore of salvation, is a long descent of God into Hell, into the desert, into the barrenness of the human heart. This descent into the abyss befits the magnitude of the love of God.

Thus, God assumes man in his contradictions, in his perverted beauty, his profaned holiness. At Matins of Holy Saturday we hear, "The one who is handsome and gracious among all mortals (Ps 45:3) appears disfigured by death, the one who gave beauty to all of nature" (Stanza 9). He presents Himself to us, but "He has no form or charm to attract us, no beauty to win our hearts" (Is 53:3).

The church fathers speak of a threefold *kenōsis* of the Son of God: becoming human, becoming sin, and dying. These three modalities of descent through the redeeming Incarnation correspond to three places: Bethlehem, the Jordan, and Golgotha. A condescending, progressive, gift of total love pursues human degeneration to the end. Each of these stages contains all the others, leads to them, or derives from them. Theological speculation certainly allows dissociation of these stages: a blessed incarnation in which suffering and death would have been excluded, or a paradisiacal incarnation inside another temporality and unfamiliar with sin. But the existential and soteriological process links these three moments in an indissoluble manner. God assumes our human nature in order to free it, to deliver us from the gangrene of sin and its final wages, death.

The return of humanity to the house of the Father, the ascent after the condescension, will occur in reverse order: death will be vanquished by the death of Christ and its sting pulled out; sin will be destroyed in its very roots, in the heart of man, by one Man who had not known sin; and humanity will be reconciled, filled with the divine Spirit, by the one who recapitulates in Himself all humans.

The mystery of the descent of the Son of God must not be enclosed in a dialectic where, according to a linear chronology, the glory of the deified and heavenly humanity of Christ would follow the *kenōsis* of His earthly life. *Kenōsis* and exaltation narrowly interpenetrate one another in all the moments of the earthly and heavenly humanity of Christ.

The Becoming Human

By becoming man, the eternal Son assumes human nature, which is beautiful and good. Even before we speak of *kenōsis,* we should not forget that human nature, in its ontology, never ceases to be beautiful and good, even in sin. The Psalms state that "of all men you are the most handsome" (Ps 45:3), and, "You have made him a little less than a god, you have crowned him with glory and beauty" (Ps 8:6).

Nonetheless, God, voluntarily tied by fallen time and space, enters into human dependency, into the need for filial and motherly tenderness. He becomes frail, impoverished, and vulnerable. He grows up in obedience. He rubs shoulders with human suffering. He knows thirst, hunger, and fatigue. The Fathers, particularly John of Damascus in the seventh century, term these experiences, "the blameless passions," or "passability," or the "natural passions." Jesus banishes all sin from these blameless passions—not through an automation or the action of a *deus ex machina,* but through the very brazier of divine love, the fire of the Holy Spirit burning in Jesus. This fire stigmatizes and consumes all temptations, every evil power, and any external evil suggestion. These can never become embedded in the citadel of the human heart of Jesus, the preeminent trinitarian dwelling. The humanity of Jesus is not abstract, impassible, or artificial: it certainly is *our* humanity, with the consequences of the sin of Adam. As St John of Damascus, cited by Fr John Meyendorff in his remarkable work *Le Christ dans la penseé byzantine* (*Christ in Eastern Christian Thought*), says: "He assumes the natural and incorruptible passions of man such as hunger, thirst, tiredness, toiling, tears, reticence before death, anguish which provokes sweat, drops of blood, and all the rest which belongs by nature to all men."[6]

But, unlike in human beings, the "passible condition" in Jesus is not a source of sin because "He suffered freely and not by necessity." "Neither hunger," John of Damascus continues, "nor thirst nor anguish, nor even death dominated Christ" or closed Him in upon Himself. Jesus remained open with the protection and power of His intense love, His arms extended to God, in prayer, on the cross, while blessing.

The Incarnation of the Son of God recalls the glorious, even paschal, aspect of His entire life. The light and the joy of the Resurrection rebound on His earthly life from the time of the Nativity, even when His divine glory is hidden. He is filled with the power of the Spirit: healings and signs follow one another, compassion is poured out, and demons are chased away. "I watched Satan fall like lightning from heaven" (Jn 10:18). The Orthodox Liturgy exalts all the moments of Jesus' earthly life from His birth, the advent of salvation itself. Even there, the cross and *kenōsis* are not forgotten or bracketed, but the *kenōsis* of Jesus, from stage to stage, is never a victory of darkness over light.

This glorious aspect of the Son of God become man also involves the total and constant unity with the Father and the Holy Spirit. On this subject, Olivier Clément quotes St Maximus the Confessor: "The Father was wholly in the Son when He fulfilled by the incarnation the mystery of our salvation. The Spirit was wholly in the Son, acting in complete unity with Him."[7] Jesus is filled with the Holy Spirit who penetrates the most intimate roots and joints, not only of His humanity but also of His divinity. Jesus is the perfect dwelling place of the Spirit, His preeminent temple. The Spirit in Jesus sighs, "Abba,

---

[6]Ed. Du Cerf (1969) 227. [See *Christ in Eastern Christian Thought*, trans. by Yves Dubois, St Vladimir's Seminary Press (1987) 165]. See also Olivier Clément who cites, in *Sources*, a beautiful text by Gregory of Nazianzus on the human sufferings of Christ and the consequences of the passivity of man, and his vulnerability to suffering (Stock, 1982, 412). [English translation by Theodore Berkely, *The Roots of Christian Mysticism*, New City, 1995].

[7]*Sources*, 42. *Roots*, 44.

Father." The Spirit of filial obedience, the Spirit of love and of perfect knowledge unites; it is this Spirit in whom Jesus is united to the Father. The compassionate God and the Spirit who leads Jesus to the temptations and trials share a unity of love, obedience, and suffering: "And at once the Spirit drove Him into the desert [. . .] and He was put to the test by Satan" (Mk 1:12); "The Spirit in whom the Son has offered Himself to the Father in a perfect sacrifice" (Heb 9:14).

The Becoming Sin

The Spirit who has dwelt in Jesus fully since His conception and birth moved Him when He reached adulthood. He prompted Him to come out of the protected environment of His domestic and hidden life in Nazareth, toward accomplishing the loving will of the Father. "The Spirit of the Lord is on me, for He has anointed me to bring the good news to the afflicted" (Lk 4:18 and Is 61), to all the poor, all the most varied forms of poverty. "Here I am! I am coming to do your will" (Heb 10:9 and Ps 110:9).

The prophetic word about the slain Lamb is accomplished at the Jordan, in the figure of the Suffering Servant, the Just One who takes upon Himself (and, at the same time, removes from us) the sin of the world. This sin of the world already is deposed in the waters of the Jordan, which thereby become symbolically black with pollution. The repentant crowd flocking toward John at the Jordan ensured this double transfer of sin and of the suffering deriving from it, first in the Jordan and then on the unblemished Lamb.

From this point of view, St Paul has a striking line: "God made Him who had no sin to be sin for us, so that in Him we might become the righteousness of God" (2 Cor 5:21). "He made Him to be sin": this terse Semitic formulary unhampered by scholastic, theological distinctions expresses the mystery of the descent of the Just One into sin, into suffering—the one whom no one could convict of sin (Jn 18:23).

Jesus takes upon Himself the transgressions of the multitude and thereby diverts the anger of God. The Adamic temptations are redone, and Satan unloads them with all his power onto Jesus, who is permeated by the Spirit and the bearer of a divine identity that remains an impenetrable mystery to the spirit of darkness. The temptations in the desert are spectacular, visible moments of the unceasing and permanent combat Jesus wages in our name against the darkness that ebbs and flows, sometimes with forceful outbursts that seem to defy life.

The Suffering and Death of Jesus

Everything here seems to blend, to merge, become confused. Satan seems to lead the dance, but actually Jesus goes forth freely to the cross. "No one takes my life from me; I lay it down of my own free will, and as I have the power to lay to down, so I have the power to take it up again" (Jn 10:18). "Do you think that I cannot appeal to my Father, who would promptly send more than twelve legions of angels?" (Mt 26:52).

Nevertheless, St Paul says, "The wages of sin is death" (Rom 6:23). By taking upon Himself the sin of the world, Jesus fulfilled these words. Death is at the same time the consequence and the antidote of sin. The Creator stated the consequence: "On the day that you eat from it, you will certainly die" (Gen 2:17). This punishment weighs upon mankind like a malediction, and Jesus turns this same malediction (or anger) upon Himself. St Paul expresses it semitically, mysteriously: "becoming a curse for us" (Gal 3:13). The entire biblical, "substitutionary," expiatory theology; the atonement for the common fault which Jesus takes upon Himself; a recovery from the disease which Jesus assumes; a liberation from the yoke exerted unjustly on the Just One; a victory over Satan the usurper: not one of these images should be isolated in the scriptural vision of redemption.

But as the antidote of sin, the death of Jesus Christ has broken in its momentum. Christ has consumed its infernal roots and extracted its sting. The seed of justice sprouts in our humanity, which Christ bears. In loving obedience to the Father, Jesus in His humanity suffered to the end. He took on the anguish, deadly sadness, lonely agony, judgment, and the passion. Jesus also confronted suffering—not as a mythological hero or a stoic, impassible under the blows, but by anticipating, accepting, and refusing to hide from them, in "a love as strong as death," as the Song of Songs says (8:6), or rather, in a love that is stronger than death.

On the cross, everything is ended, all is accomplished: the Lord reigns, the prince of the world is thrown out, the kingdom of Satan is abolished. Voracious Hades devours the Master of life but is unable to contain Him, for nothing in Jesus belongs to hell by right: no mark of shadow or of sin. The full and pure light of love illuminates hell and swallows up the source of all suffering. Let us not be afraid to speak of the death of Jesus—and of His resurrection—as a sacrifice because the sacrifice is an essential aspect of the love of the Father and the Son. The Father required no sacrifice to appease His wrath—this image of the Father's anger is secondary in the Bible. Rather, this is a sacrifice of offering, of descent and then of ascent, in search of the lost sheep. It is a sacrifice of consecration, of the exorcising of human nature corrupted by sin, of the healing of humanity sick through sin, and of the consolation of humanity bewildered in loneliness, far from the sources of living water. Jesus reaches and heals the intimate depths of humanity. This is a sacrifice of reintegration by which all of creation is brought back to the Father.

As Olivier Clément writes, "Because of the ontological unity of Christ with the whole human race, the sacrifice was a bloody crucifixion. United with us in being and in love, Christ took on Himself all the hatred, rebellion, derision, despair—'My God, my God, why hast thou forsaken me?'—all the murders, all the suicides, all the tortures, all the agonies of all humanity throughout all time and all space. In all these, Christ bled, suffered, and cried out in anguish and in desolation. But as He suffered in a human way, so was He trustful in a human way: 'Father into thy hands I commit my spirit.' At that moment death is swallowed up in life, the abyss of hatred is lost in the bottomless depths of love."[8]

The descent into hell inaugurates the ascent of Jesus to the Father in our humanity, which is indissoluble and nuptially linked to Him.

[8] *Sources*, 43. *Roots*, 44.

The risen body of the Savior carries the marks of the Passion. However, these wounds and injuries are no longer flowing with blood and pain, but with light and life, like so many sources of the Spirit. Call to mind the words of Jesus committing His Spirit to the Father, or the outflow of blood and water from His pierced side, or the touching of Thomas (Jn 20:17) and of the other apostles (Lk 24:39). These communications of the Spirit announce and anticipate Pentecost. "Give your blood and receive the Spirit," the Fathers said. In Jesus Christ, blood is the major locus of the Spirit. Through the blood of the Passion, the Spirit is communicated already and is anticipated as an awaited promise—"You will receive the promise of the Father," to be given finally in the one and permanent Pentecost of the Church.

From henceforth and forever, the wind of the Spirit blows upon the world. Above all, it is the place of the presence of Christ: "Henceforth the world is breached by an enclave of non-death. From now on we can enter into the resurrection, make it with our own character, and proceed by means of Christ's humanity to His divinity."[9] In His earthly life Jesus was the place of the Spirit of God, His favorite place, total and unique. Today, in the time of the Church, the Spirit is the place of the presence of Jesus. He is a stream of new life flowing over our mortal bodies, a place of presence diffused in the sacramental Church, in the sacramental human hearts.

The Bride of the Lamb

In the Spirit, the Church carries on the work of mercy, of healing, of compassion, of forgiveness by the Lord. All the sacraments of the Church—notably confession and the anointing of the sick—and all the benedictions and intercessions are irruptions of the divine power of healing, of forgiveness, and of consolation.

Just as the whole earthly life of our Savior and the humbling of the Eternal Son are filled with glory and radiant with life, wisdom, and love, so does the Church, the Bride of the Lamb, perpetuate the

[9]Ibid. 52. Ibid. 55.

kenōsis of the Risen One, not only in the earthly members of the Church but also in Himself. The implosion of the Eucharist makes people contemporary to the events of salvation. Reciprocally, our sins and divisions tear the seamless garment of the Savior and also disfigure His face of light. But our sufferings always ascend to the throne of God, to the throne of the divine, blessed Trinity. Moreover, the Church and its children follow the path of the Master, the way of the cross, and of sacrificial love.

With regard to the redeeming and salutary character of suffering itself, it is obvious that an inalienable residue of "non-sense," of negativity, of scandal remains linked to suffering. For suffering may cause degradation, alienation, and hardening. Sin itself may result from suffering that was refused.

Beyond the penal concepts conveyed in the Old Testament, the mystery of suffering appears, and the pure Lamb of Deutero-Isaiah intensely expresses it. Only a voluntary, unblemished victim, a suffering substitute, acquires a sufficient sacramental value, through which the anger of God wears out and becomes dull.

Through the sacrifice of Jesus Christ, the image of God in the human being is rebuilt, and the very nature of man is healed. "Christ," John Paul II says, "has uplifted human suffering even to give it a redemptive value." The prophets—by anticipation, the apostles—by inheritance, the martyrs of all times, and the saints of our day partake of the redemptive suffering of the Savior (Col 1:24). The saints have imitated the unblemished, defenseless Lamb and, like Him, have become vulnerable to love, violent in love, stronger than death. The countless suffering of the living and the deceased members of the Church witness to the Lamb. It is in Jesus alone that our suffering also becomes a sacrament; it becomes this to the extent that our hearts and bodies are slowly and painfully purified of the germs of passions—sins that dwell in us and render us resistant to love.

Having said this, it is difficult to speak of beneficial suffering. We can accept suffering ourselves and witness to it in a spirit of surrender to God and in the certainty of His loving Providence but without expounding on it. It is dangerous to speak of suffering as a divine means of salvation. Great discernment, tact, compassion, and prayerful and loving sharing are needed in order not to objectify the suffering of others into a divine law or a necessary pedagogy. The first love of the Father is revealed only at the return of the prodigal son to the house of the Father. Only then did the trials of the son in a faraway country acquire a beneficial and salutary character.

The Merciful Heart

Faced with the suffering of others and with sin, the Christian will, above all, have a look of compassion, a word of consolation, and a gesture of healing and of forgiveness—a look that reflects the gaze of Christ. "If anyone," St John says, "is well off in worldly possessions, and sees a brother in need but closes his heart to him, how can the love of God be remaining in him" (1 Jn 3:17)? This is echoed by the words of St James: "Suppose a brother or sister is without clothes and daily food. If anyone say to him, 'Go, I wish you well' . . . but does nothing about his physical needs, what good is it" (Jas 2:16)? The first urgency in the presence of suffering and grief is to relieve it (Mt 25:31).

In our own lives, Jesus is our living and permanent reference. He is at the same time the giver of the Spirit and the gift of the Spirit. In Him the heart serves the apprenticeship of prayer and, through it, the apprenticeship of love. I learn love when the mysterious transfer of my "me" to the centrality of Christ occurs; when "I no longer live, but Christ lives in me" (Gal 2:20); when it is no longer I who pray but the Spirit who prays in me; and when it is no longer I who love, but the Father who loves in me.

To confront the vision of suffering and of evil in this manner is to continue what Jesus did. It is to let Christ live and resonate in us, to let Him pray in us, while being fortified certainly by the Holy Spirit. For the Holy Spirit is not only the Spirit of victory and of the resurrection; He is also, and as much, the Spirit of passion and of compassion; He is the one whom ancient liturgies called "the royal purple of Emmanuel," the witness to the sufferings of Christ.

When we follow the path of Jesus, we learn how to offer our own hearts to God. It is then that the heart opens and fortifies itself in the spirit of compassion. The human being is able to be filled with the misery of the world, to carry it on his or her shoulders, and to lay it down before the throne of God. But our hearts are weak and inconstant. Given up to ourselves, we tend to close up, to protect ourselves from suffering—which is always too great—to ignore or forget it. Nonetheless, this same heart is called to love, to compassion, to mercy. It can only respond to this call by merging into the heart of Jesus. That requires, as a precondition, a purification, an exorcising of the evil that is in us, in all forms. The evil in the world can be exorcised and burned only to the extent that the roots of evil which lie in our own hearts are exorcised, banished, and burned, consumed in the face-to-face with Jesus, with His Name, His Cross, and His Spirit. "This type of spirit can be driven out only by praying and by fasting" (Mt 17:22).

Thus we are back at the starting point of this meditation: the inextricable mixture of "passion-suffering," of degeneration, and of "passion-sin," sin that is at the same time collective and personal, an enslavement to hidden but venomous forces. "Go and sin no more," Jesus tells the paralytic at the pool of Bethesda (Jn 5:14) and to the adulterous woman (Jn 8:11). "My child, your sins are forgiven," Jesus says as a preliminary to healing. Through divine forgiveness, the human being receives an in-depth healing.

Thus, absolved from our sins, healed of our sinful passions, and strong only in our natural passions that have become irreproachable as so many channels of grace, we are able to turn to the image of the divine Lamb and bring the sinful passions of humanity to the attention of His gaze: a look of tenderness, of forgiveness, of hope.

CHAPTER TWO

LOVE FOR ENEMIES IN THE GOSPELS

I t is not easy to speak of the love for enemies. To speak of it, one must live it, and who of us can say that he or she lives this commandment of the Lord: "Love your enemies, and pray for those who persecute you" (Mt 5:44)?

Going beyond the Mosaic Law

The Sermon on the Mount, Matthew 5 and following, contrasts the commandments of the Mosaic Law to the commandments of Jesus, "the new Moses." In the Gospels and in the entire New Testament, we find a contrast—which is not a conflict, but rather a going beyond—between the ancient law and the new law.

Before even speaking about the evangelical preaching, we must evoke these "two *Moshes*" (*Moshe* is Hebrew for "Moses"). Moses inclines before the Lord at Tabor, giving first place to him. Like John the Baptist, Moses must decrease so that Jesus might increase. John the Evangelist also recalls this: "The Law was given through Moses, grace and truth have come through Jesus Christ" (Jn 1:17).

The work of salvation is altogether a slow, painful pedagogy. On several occasions in the Sermon on the Mount, Jesus says: "You have heard . . . But I tell you . . ." Moses is not mentioned. What is repeated only is "You have heard" (*on vous a dit*). This "*on*" is an impersonal expression that covers the written law of the Pentateuch, the Torah, and the oral law that encompasses the current concepts of the Judaic mentality up to the time of the Lord. In fact, the words of the Lord— "You have heard how it was said, you will love your neighbor and hate your enemy" (Mt 5:43)— are not found literally in the Pentateuch. No text gives exactly this phrase: "You will hate your enemy." Here and there in the Old Testament the question of hatred occurs. The psalmist exclaims: "How I hate them, O Lord, that hate thee! I am cut to the quick when they oppose thee; I hate them with undying hatred" (Ps 139:21–22); and Psalm 137 cries, "By the rivers of Babylon . . . a blessing on anyone who seizes your babies and shatters them against a rock."

"Love your enemies, pray for those who persecute you." The commandment of the New Testament cannot be separated from the overall teaching of the Gospels. A few verses earlier, the Lord had said, "If you are offering your gift at the altar . . . first go and be reconciled to your brother . . . ; settle matters quickly with your adversary" (Mt 5:24–25). The text uses two different terms to designate the same person: "brother" and "adversary." This clearly indicates an absence of boundary, in real life, between brotherhood and enmity. In a twinkling of an eye one can pass from the one to the other, and conversely. We are moving beyond the *lex talionis* (law of retaliation): "an eye for an eye, a tooth for a tooth."

Jesus does mention Moses a little further down, particularly in Matthew's chapter on the indissolubility of marriage: "[You have heard that] Moses permitted you to divorce your wives because your hearts were hard. But it was not this way from the beginning, I tell you . . ." (Mt 19:8). Thus we are allowed to retain in this "You have heard, but I tell you" the teaching of the Mosaic Law. In the face of the hardening of the hearts, Jesus is compelled, so to speak, to give legislation and more stringent pedagogical rules. Nonetheless, these mark a progress in comparison with the neighboring civilizations, if we think of the law of retaliation and human sacrifice in particular.

The Father's Forgiveness

A second essential point is found in the Lord's Prayer: "Forgive us our trespasses as we forgive those who trespass against us." By addressing ourselves to the Father we can find and receive forgiveness, and we are able to forgive. Precisely on the cross, Jesus prays the Father to forgive. It is not Jesus who forgives, but the Father. The Gospel of Matthew says, "Be perfect, therefore, as your heavenly Father is perfect" (Mt 5:45); and the Gospel of Luke: "Be merciful, just as your heavenly Father is merciful" (Lk 6:36). We can say that the Father is the highest source of forgiveness because we are all His children. All of us are called to become His children, and this fraternity can pass only through forgiveness.

The Germ of Evil in the Heart

The standard concepts of "brother," "neighbor," "adversary," or "enemy" should be reconsidered in light of the new law. There is no watertight barrier between them, but a passage from the one to the other. From the beginning, the law of sin is spread out over the entire earth like gangrene. It penetrates into the inmost human heart, where it breaks the integrity and inner unity. Man is divided, alienated from himself, from God, from his brothers; he becomes an enemy to himself, of God, of his brothers.

The history of Cain and Abel, like that of Joseph and his brothers, is at the same time decisive and emblematic of all our fraternities, all our natural relations. Ancestral sin, even before the murder of Abel by Cain had already introduced enmity like a universal germ of hostility in human relationships. Friendship and natural love, whether of a parental, fraternal, or conjugal order, sometimes hide hatreds and tenacious resentments behind a smiling face. Let us recall the words of the Lord on the whitewashed graves. They concern not only the Pharisees of His time, but also all of humanity.

The Fight against the Enemy

Behind the mystery of evil and hatred, the profile of the Adversary stands out, of Satan—which means "adversary" in Hebrew. He is the one who personifies hatred, who is the preeminent enemy, the enemy of people and the enemy of God, the one who spreads evil in the hearts: "while everyone was sleeping, his enemy came and sowed weeds (among the wheat)" (Mt 13.25). Jesus confronts this power and fights against it throughout His entire earthly course, from Bethlehem, to the desert of temptation, to Golgotha. He strikes this power dead through His own death on the cross: "I saw Satan fall like lightning from heaven" (Lk 10:18). "Now is the time for judgment on this world; now the Prince of this world will be driven out" (Jn 1:31). St Paul, who already starts a theological reflection, declares: "He Himself is our peace . . . He has destroyed the dividing wall of hostility. He abolished in His flesh hatred to make peace" (Eph 2:14–16). "While we were still sinners, Christ died for us" (Rom 5:8). Thus, there is a reversal of relationships. Jesus does not wait until we come to him. As long as we are still sinners, as long as we are "under the wrath of God," enemies of God, and crushed under the burden, Jesus comes to us, sent by the Father. For "God—that is, the Father—so loved the world that He gave His one and only Son" (Jn 3:16).

This personification of evil and hatred in Satan and in his angels allows us to appropriate some of the most relentless and cruel texts of the Old Testament, by giving a spiritual reading of them. I am thinking in particular of the last two verses of the psalm quoted earlier (Ps 136:8–9). On the vigils of the Sundays before Lent, one feels like conjuring away these bothersome words. In their spiritual reading, the Fathers teach us to see in the children of Babylon or the children of Egypt, a symbol of sin, of hatred, of Satan. Thus we try to smash all these offshoots of evil and sin that try to live in us against the Rock, Christ. Provided they are interpreted in their spiritual sense, such words do remain in the light of the work of Christ.

The Gift of the Holy Spirit

Jesus' teaching on forgiving trespasses and love for our enemies finds its ultimate, full truth in the prayer of the Crucified One for His executioners: "Father, forgive them, for they do not know what they are doing" (Lk 23:34). Only the forgiveness of trespasses breaks the infernal circle of hatred and vengeance. The law of retaliation (*lex talionis*) is abolished. But the new law remains foolishness for the world because it is the language of the cross (1 Cor 1:2). Christ is our peace, the place of pacification, the maker of the peace of the Beatitudes, for He is the only one who is truly peaceful and we must penetrate His peace. We will then become the children of God and will inherit the earth.

Jesus gives us gifts before His Passion, with the promise of the Holy Spirit: "The Counselor will be with you" (Jn 14:16). "He will remind you of everything I have said to you" (Jn 14:26). "Receive the Holy Spirit" (Jn 20:22). Jesus is present in us, through the power of the Holy Spirit. "Anyone who has faith in me, will do what I have been doing. He will do even greater things than these" (Jn 14:12).

To the extent that we enter into the mystery of Christ, who died for us when we were all sinners and under the wrath of God, our hearts in our deepest being is transformed. The heart, once inhabited by the forces of darkness and hatred, becomes the dwelling place of the Holy Spirit. It is no longer I who live—this detestable I—but Christ who lives in me (Gal 2:20). He is the one who lives, who loves, who forgives. He is the one who prays and intercedes. Jesus on the cross makes heavenly intercession, as the one whom the Epistle of the Hebrews and the entire Christian tradition calls "the high priest." Essentially the risen Christ prays that we might enter into His prayer and forgive. In the breath of the Spirit who sighs in us, "Abba, Father," He is the one who is poured out in our hearts. This is the gift of Pentecost, the gift of tongues, the anti-Babel.

According to St Paul, "God has poured out love into our hearts by the Holy Spirit, whom He has given us" (Rom 5:5). He is the one who teaches us all things, especially how to pray for our enemies. He is the one who prays in our hearts, and we should prick up our inner ear to perceive His sighs, to let ourselves be invaded, modeled in the image of the Crucified One. Then we might repeat the words of Staretz St Silouan that derive quite naturally from the gospel and the entire doctrine of the New Testament: "The Holy Spirit teaches that one should love one's enemies so much that one will have compassion on them as one would on one's own children. The one who does not love his enemies does not have the grace of God."[1]

---

[1]Archimandrite Sophrony, *Starets Silouan, Moine du Mont-Athos*, ed. Présence (1973) 260. [English translation by Rosemary Edmunds, *St Silouan the Athonite*, St Vladimir's Seminary Press (1999).]

CHAPTER THREE

THE MYSTERY OF FORGIVENESS

The Lord's Prayer, in general, and according to my personal experience, is the most difficult prayer there is. One often has the habit of reciting it in a drone—but it is not a prayer one can "recite." The Lord's Prayer in the eucharistic Liturgy is sung or uttered in community after the *epiclesis*, after the invocation of the Holy Spirit—when the Holy Spirit, the Spirit of fire, has descended upon the gifts, the bread and the wine, and upon the community to transform all the persons present into the Body and Blood of Christ. Only then is Our Father said and lived in all its fullness, in all its power, in all its audacity: "Vouchsafe, O Master, that with boldness and without condemnation, we may dare to call upon thee . . ."[1] This word *parrhēsia*, which introduces the Our Father, has a triple meaning: boldness, familiarity, confidence. These elements go together.

"Forgive Us Our Trespasses"

In that context, we can enter into one of the most difficult petitions of this prayer: "And forgive us our trespasses as we forgive those who trespass against us."[2] The literal translation of this central petition of the Our Father should be: "Forgive us our debts as we forgive our debtors." Exegetes note here a slight variant between the Gospel of Luke and that of Matthew, the second being longer than the first. In

---

[1]Proclamation of the priest before the choir and the people sing or recite the Our Father in the Orthodox Divine Liturgy.

[2]I first wanted to say *the most* difficult, but I will say *one of the most* difficult because the term Our Father is already hard to pronounce: how can we enter and lift up ourselves to this mystery of God who dwells in an inaccessible light, and call Him "Father"?

Matthew we read: "Forgive us our debts, *as* we have also forgiven our debtors" (Mt 6:12); in Luke: "Forgive us our sins, *for* we also forgive everyone who sins against us" (Lk 11:4). Is there a real difference, a gulf between the "for," which indicates a relation of causality and the "as," which perhaps implies more of an analogy? There actually is no great difference between the two because the basic problem remains: if we expect God to forgive us to the extent of our own forgiveness, it is a vain hope because we ourselves are not able to forgive. We may refer to certain passages of the Old Testament, particularly the text of Ecclesiasticus, which says essentially: "How can we ask for God's forgiveness, if we ourselves do not forgive these who owe us?" (Sir 28: 3).

The literal text of the Our Father does not speak of forgiveness, but of a remission of debt. This is the true translation, literal and rigorous, which is that of the Slavonic[3] and to which we should return.

God's Forgiveness Is First

The entire context of the Bible compels us not to make mutual forgiveness the condition for the forgiveness of God, but, quite to the contrary, to see the necessary consequence in it. One of the fundamental parables, in which we discover that God's forgiveness is first, sheds light on the Our Father: A man who owed ten thousand talents—a vast sum of money—to his master, threw himself at the feet of his master and asked for a delay. The master set him free and granted him a remission of his entire debt (Mt 18:23–35).

We encounter this fundamental fact everywhere—the priority, the primacy of the forgiveness of God. St Paul also speaks of it in the Epistle to the Romans: "At just the right time, when we were still powerless, Christ died for the ungodly . . . While we were sinners, Christ died for us. Very rarely will anyone die for a good man, but Christ demonstrated His love for us in this: while we were still sinners, Christ died for us—that is the profound meaning of forgiveness" (Rom 5:6ff). St Paul confirms in the Epistle to the Ephesians: "Be kind and compassionate to one another, forgiving each other, just as in Christ God

[3]Russian liturgical language.

forgave you" (Eph 4:32). Let us note that "as God forgave you" is in the definitive past: in Christ we are forgiven once and for all. St Paul repeats this essential fact of the redemption of Christ in the Epistle to the Colossians: "Bear with each other and forgive whatever grievances you may have against one another. Forgive as the Lord forgave you" (Col 3:13).

In all these passages, the forgiveness of God comes *first*. Certainly, we can ask ourselves, "Is there not a contradiction, then, between this priority and the words of the Our Father?" "Forgive us . . . as we forgive those who trespass against us"?

Going more deeply into this question, we discover two degrees regarding the forgiveness of God. The first is universal and absolute, nontemporal and permanent, for all times and for all places: God has saved us, once and for all—this is the great doctrine of St Paul. God desires not the death of the sinners, but that they may be converted and live.

This pardon of God is unconditional, for God loved us when we were still sinners. He even died for us (Rom 5:8). Forgiveness is given to us and we only have "to enter into it." God is victorious; we only have to penetrate into that victory.

But—and this is the second degree of forgiveness—through the action of the Holy Spirit we are called to be collaborators with the work of God by assuming this mystery and this achievement, the fruit of the forgiveness of God. When we reject our brothers, we reject the forgiveness of God. Universal forgiveness is offered but not imposed. The human being remains free—this is the great mystery of the Christian faith—in the presence of the love of God, the forgiveness of God, the light of God, which we may accept or reject. Thus, our refusal of God is part of the mystery of His love.

The Prayer of Christ on the Cross

To conclude this New Testament panorama, it is proper to recall the prayer of Christ on the cross: "Father, forgive them, for they do not now what they are doing" (Lk 23:34). Jesus grants not a pardon, but

offers a prayer to the Father. These words of the Crucified One resonate throughout the centuries until the end of time. These words are
words of the supreme reconciliation with the Father, the filial intercession for this world that "God so loved" (Jn 3:16), the prayer of the
New Abel whose blood "cries out to the Father" (Gen 4:10). This
request for God's forgiveness is the summit of Jesus' blood offering.

This prayer of Jesus on the cross encompasses, embraces all times
and all space, from the beginning to the end of the ages. Being in solidarity with His executioners, we all are concerned with this prayer of
forgiveness that Christ addresses to the Father. The slightest refusal of
God, indeed the smallest rejection of His love, unites us with those
who tempted Christ during His life, and with those who crucified
Him. Thus, this prayer of Christ is truly an *epiclesis* to the Father.
Christ does not declare "I forgive you," but He refers to the one who
is higher than Him: "My Father is greater than I." Likewise, He
addresses His Father before His Passion: "I will ask the Father, and He
will give you another counselor, the Spirit of truth . . . He will testify
about me" (Jn 14:16; 15:26). At Golgotha, Jesus continues to beseech
the Father to forgive people.

The forgiveness of the Father descends on the world, for it is the
Father who is wounded. Here we find a theme that is fundamental in
the church fathers, that of the Father's compassion, meaning "suffering with." The Father is not insensitive before the passion, the suffering, and the decay of humanity that removes itself from Him at an
infinite speed. The Father suffers from a "love wound," and the high
point of His suffering is the death of the Son He sends into the world,
this world He "so loved." Until the end of time, the sign of the forgiveness of God will be the gift of the Holy Spirit.

The Dimensions of Sin

But what is forgiveness? John the Baptist's statement "Look! There is
the Lamb of God; it is He who takes away the sin of the world" (Jn
1:29) is borrowed from the fourth song of Isaiah: "Behold, the Lamb
of God" (Is 53). God takes upon Himself the sin of the world: the evil,

our transgressions, our sufferings, our wounds, our bruises, our degeneration, and our entire condition. In the Old Testament, sin is not merely individual deeds, no matter how heavy; sin (in the singular) also has a universal, generic meaning, which refers to the global condition of the Fall, of evil, of suffering, of slavery, of corruption, of mortality in which all of humanity is plunged in solidarity.

Behind sin, there is a personal power—this is the great doctrine of St Irenaeus of Lyons. Sin is not merely a state of being. It is a personified power that depersonalizes and alienates, which seeks to subdue and destroy humanity. *Diabolos*, the one who divides, dissociates, and breaks up, is the agent of sin: "Simon, Simon, Satan has asked to sift you as wheat" (Lk 22:31), that is "to disperse you." Conversely, Jesus died "to gather together the scattered children of God, and bring them into one" (Jn 11:52).

Satanic dividing is always threefold: compromising and breaking the "communing" character of man, it isolates him with respect to God, to men, and to himself. Before God, the heavens close, and God becomes far away, His face becomes harsh. Sources of divine grace seem to run dry, and man becomes an orphan, lost and famished in a "distant country" (Jn 15:13). Towards his brothers, man becomes a wolf for man—*homo homini lupus*, as a Latin proverb says. The fratricide of Cain, the tower of Babel, the law of retaliation become the biblical archetypes of the barrier of hate, of incomprehension and vengeance, that is erected between people and compromises the brotherly communion for which people were created.

Finally, most seriously, the human being disintegrates, losing integrity and the profound unity of being. The deep heart, the immaterial place in the image of God, though indestructible, becomes alienated, seriously overshadowed, darkened, and locked up in its own depth. The human being becomes a stranger to his or her identity and ultimate vocation, roaming like a suffering soul between heaven and earth. In this state of multiple dissociation, the human being is at the same time a victim of possessive satanic powers and enslaved to his or her own desires and passions. Additionally, the human person harbors the seeds of death; he or she is ill since birth and destined to die.

Enslavement and sickness do not make humanity entirely irre-
sponsible, despite St Paul's lament: "For what I want to do I do not do,
but what I hate I do" (Rom 7:19). From the beginning to the end of
time, God addresses Himself to the "Cain" in each one of us: "Cain,
what have you done to your brother?" (Gen 4:9). What have you done
also to this intimate voice of the Spirit who sighs in your depths, to
this Beggar for love who knocks tirelessly at the door of your heart?
(Rev 3:20). Responsibility and guilt remain because the image of God
continues to glow in the depths.

Elimination of Sin and Healing

When God forgives, He wipes away the sin, and He heals the under-
lying wound. What was, He renders nonexistent, He forgets and turns
away; He does not consider the sin. Further, He creates a new heart
(Ps 51 [50]:12). He is the Lamb that takes away the sin and who has
taken upon Himself the sin and the wounds of men. Only God can
bring about such forgiveness. Only God can erase the sin and render
it nonexistent. Man cannot truly forgive by himself: he does not have
the strength for it because the wound in him is too big; it continues
to bleed and cause suffering. Only God can forgive.

Forgiveness is the mystery of the love of the Father. This is why, at
the decisive moment, at the moment one may call the ultimate temptation—that of the Savior on the cross—where God sees the entire
world gathered together in one point, Christ can only address Himself
to the Father. This forgiveness is an integral part of the mystery of
redemption, of the renewal, of salvation, of the new creation. Nonetheless, the Gospels teach us: "But that you may know that the Son of Man
has the authority to forgive sins, He said to the paralytic, I tell you, get
up, take your mat and go home"(Mk 2:10). St John reveals to us that the
Son of man has received from the Father the power to judge, and that
this judgment is not only a judgment of condemnation but also a judgment of forgiveness, of salvation and healing.

God is a God of forgiveness. Several essential passages in the Old
Testament, as in the theophany of Exodus (3:46) where God reveals

Himself to Moses, clearly show this: "Yahweh, Yahweh, God of tenderness and compassion, slow to anger, rich in faithful love and constancy, maintaining His faithful love to thousands, forgiving fault, crime and sin, yet letting nothing go unchecked, and punishing the parent's fault in the children and the grandchildren to the third and fourth generation." The contrast is important: if the atonement or the punishment goes to the third and fourth generation, forgiveness, then, extends over thousands of generations. The psalm read at vespers recalls: "Yahweh is tenderness and pity, slow to anger and rich in faithful love" (Ps 103 [102]), and also the book of Jonah recounts the prophet announcing the divine punishment on Nineveh but God taking pity on the people of this city.

Let Us Lift up Our Hearts

What, then, does forgiveness mean for us? It is to let God heal the wound of our own heart. When the heart is wounded, we cannot forgive because the suffering and the resentment are too great. To forgive is a gift of God, a true miracle of transformation in our own hearts; we cannot heal ourselves. This is why it is important to link the mystery of forgiveness to the prayer of the heart.

When we hear the words of the priest at the eucharistic liturgy, "Let us lift up our hearts" and the response of the choir, "We lift them up unto the Lord," what happens at that moment? What does it mean "to lift up one's heart to God?" This can be understood in the sense of forgetting all that is earthly, human, secular, and of turning to God in a relationship of absolute verticality, of prayer, adoration, and total supplication. That, however, is only a way of perception because, whether we like it or not, our heart is a universe. Our heart is wider than the world because it contains it; it knows that the world does not know this mystery it carries within. When our hearts are filled with everything that make up our existence, our joys, our sorrows, all our loves, all our hatred and sufferings, what can we do? We are not able to tear all this from our hearts. Thus, we can only lift up our hearts to God. Just as we expose the sick part of our body to radiation that can heal it, so do we lift up our sick hearts and ask the Lord to penetrate them; we ask Him to enter into our sick and beseeching hearts with all His power, His grace, His love, with all the presence, the light and the fire of the Spirit to consume what must be, to transform and recreate what must remain for the kingdom.

St Paul says it well: "The wicked will not inherit the kingdom of God" (1 Cor 6:9). The very fact of lifting up our hearts implies necessarily a purification, a cauterization, a healing. If we have hatred, it is burned gradually, consumed. It melts like snow in the sun. All the barriers we have created and put up against one another dwindle gradually and disappear.

Thus, when we lift up our hearts, we lift up our joys and our hatreds, our friends and our enemies. Lifting up one's heart is a true baptism of the heart—a baptism in which the heart will die again and rise with everything it contains. As St Paul said: "[Christ] has destroyed the dividing wall of hostility" (Eph 2:14) between those who are near and those who are far, between heaven and earth; "There is neither Jew nor Greek, male or female" (Gal 3:28). Christ has brought us all together. When we lift up our hearts to Christ, the wall of hatred is destroyed. This is the baptism of the heart, the oblation of our hearts. At this depth a true forgiveness can be achieved—that is, not only a forgetting, but a discovery, an entering into the love of Christ. It is only in Christ and in His prayer—in which we are immersed—that our forgiveness can be real and effective.

One last point seems important to me. Very often, when I reflect on the manner of forgiving, I discover that when *I* forgive, I view myself to be at the center of things: it is *I* who forgive, for it is *me* who has been wounded. When I forgive, it is always the *me* that is praised. Here it would be good to recall the parable of Christ about the beam and the mote: "Why do you look at the speck of sawdust in your brother's eye and pay no attention to the plank in your own eye?" (Lk 6:41). Let us learn how to implement this conversion of the eye: what we consider as an object of forgiveness in others may be rather ludicrous in connection with what we ourselves owe.

Repentance: The Key to Forgiveness

For who am I not to forgive? Am I not myself "born in sin" as the psalm says (51 [50]:5)? I am indebted for each moment, every instant of my life where I turn away from God, where I let darkness or hatred enter in me. I am infinitely indebted toward all people: each time I impede the action of the Holy Spirit who works for my sanctification, I introduce a little or much darkness into the entire world. As indebted to all people, would not my real resolution be to ask forgiveness, even before offering forgiveness? When I ask for forgiveness while viewing myself as "the least of men and the chief sinner,"[4] the forgiveness of the other assumes another resonance. Therefore I cannot forgive unless I ask forgiveness from all and each. This is the preliminary and inner dimension of forgiveness. When I forgive, it is still the *me* that is at the center. Conversely, when I ask for forgiveness, I break this proud *me*; the forgiveness of the neighbor, or of the one whose neighbor I am, becomes necessary.

The mystery of repentance is the first work of the Holy Spirit, which is to bring us to recognize ourselves as sinners, aliens, and orphans. "Give your blood and receive the Spirit," a patristic adage states. The Spirit descends on the world in tongues of fire, in dew of living water to quench the thirsty, in healing the wounds of sin, in leading the lost sheep to the house of the Father, when I discover myself—and me alone—as a sinner and guilty (I Tim 1:15). I ask forgiveness from all and each, but above all from God who alone can forgive: "Who can forgive sins but God alone?" (Mk 2:7).

[4]Prayer recited before Holy Communion in the Orthodox Liturgy. See 1 Tim 1:15.

The Liturgy of the Heart

CHAPTER FOUR

THE PRAYER OF THE HEART
AND SUFFERING

To sustain the vision, the drama, the reality of suffering, all of us are compelled to find the true method, the strength, and the grace not to harden or destroy ourselves when faced with it. This fulcrum that would allow us to raise the world is for us Christians the Lord Jesus. He is the one who lets us draw from the infinite source of His compassion; it is through Him that we can find refuge in the bosom of the Father, to be adorned with mercy, to fill ourselves with the compassion of the Holy Spirit.

What is the role of the prayer of the heart in this process? Right away, when we speak of the prayer of the heart, we should make a distinction between two things. On the one hand, certain specific techniques have their historical, methodological, and pedagogical significance, and belong to certain surroundings, which require a certain way of life. On the other, St Thérèse of Lisieux identified it very simply as, "to take refuge in the arms of Jesus," that is, to turn toward Him with our entire being. We do not have to discuss the prayer of the heart; we have to discover it and speak about it from our own experience.

Our Own Suffering and the Suffering of the Other

Without entering into the various types of suffering—basically there exists one's own suffering and the suffering of another. Sooner or later, we must serve our apprenticeship in accepting and assuming our own suffering, climbing a path to God through it. It is never easy, but it is possible and even necessary to decide to ground ourselves on the one who has taken upon Himself not merely our sin, but also our suffering.

Faced with the suffering of the other, the first basic point is recalling that the human being is, by nature, by virtue of vocation, a "being of communion," a sharing being and—when faced with what the world has become and what the human being has undergone—a being of compassion. Etymologically, *compatir* (to commiserate) means "to suffer with," that is, to share the suffering of the other, to take it upon oneself.

The second basic point is realizing that sin, fear, and all their consequences—hatred, violence, egoism, egocentrism, and all their visible or subtle forms—make us strangers three times: to others, to ourselves, and to God. We cannot open ourselves to God without opening ourselves to those nearby. We cannot let the suffering and the needs of others enter into us without seeking strength and love in God Himself. Nor can we accomplish all that if we do not strive to be unified inwardly, through purification and the way of life that God imposes. Prayer of the heart presupposes and signifies this entire mystery of the human heart.

This inner work of preparation, of strengthening, of human and spiritual maturity, is an essential prerequisite. When the degree of horror and of suffering is too high—I am thinking in particular of certain forms of illness, of torture, of wars, of the unimaginable amount of suffering our century knows—this can become unbearable.

Under these circumstances, if a person wants to remain open, sensitive, and receptive to these sufferings, he or she runs several risks: the risk of either self-destruction or—if desiring to remain alive—the risk of developing a hard shell for protection and security or of developing adverse reactions such as sadism and cruelty. No one is immunized against this. Not one of these dangers is entirely and totally alien to us. All of us, saints as well as sinners, walk along abysses of hatred and evil, which only may find a complicity in us. These abysses and these forces appeal to us without exception. We could not even speak of them with a certain degree of truthfulness if we did not know—alas!—their tastes, their smells. Here I am thinking of the experiences of the saints: Seraphim of Sarov, who gave us premonitions of his nightly struggle; or St Thérèse of Lisieux tempted by atheism; or great Christian novelists such as Bernanos and Dostoevsky, who, in the abyss and the underground of human being, discovered simultaneously the root of unbelief *and* the mystery of Christ.

Living the Life in Christ

We face permanent dilemmas: Where do we find the strength to resist this psychic and spiritual destruction? Even more, where do we find the strength to sustain, console, and share? How do we stay alive? How not to harden or destroy oneself? How do we cry and suffer with the one who cries and suffers?

Prayer of the heart, not as a panacea, but as a "master key," is a tool that has stood the test. What is important is not the "technique" of this prayer, but a deep life as a believer. At the ground level of being and life, Christians faced with suffering find the proper attitude. Living the life of Christ, letting oneself be penetrated by His Spirit, by His breath of mercy, constitutes Christianity. According to the Bible, that means acquiring the bowels of compassion and tenderness of the Father. According to the second chapter of Philippians, it presupposes having the same feelings as Jesus Christ, not in the sense of mimicry or external imitation, but a true "transfer" on a plane more important and fundamental than the psychological level. A transfer of presence, of life center, of grace and love must operate in us so that we might live in Christ, and Christ might live in us. Certainly, this transfer operates in a global, constant, and progressive manner, through the sacramental life, love, prayer, and faith. For us Christians, the Church is the place of apprenticeship of this transfer: its entire pedagogy, its sacramental and liturgical transmission, its spiritual methodology, and its ascetic experience of the inner life, what the Fathers call the unseen warfare against the passions.

Prayer of the heart is to be placed within this global framework, this unified context of the life in Christ. *The Life in Christ* is the title of one of the most beautiful works of a fourteenth-century spiritual mystic, St Nicholas Cabasilas,[1] who teaches us about the Christian life through the sacraments, the deepening of prayer, and mercy. *My Life in Christ*, a book by St John of Kronstadt,[2] a great Russian spiritual author of the beginning of the twentieth century, also presents a meditation on the life in Christ. Prayer of the heart is not merely a mode or a practice among others, but a central reality through which the human being truly rediscovers the secret of his or her existence.

The Heart: The Seat of the Spiritual Life

According to the anthropology of the Bible and the most authentic spirituality of the West as well as of the East, the concept of the heart does not refer merely to the affective life in the purely banal and human sense of the term, as one of the components of human life. In the Bible, the heart appears as the preeminent seat of the spiritual life: the place of the presence of God, but also the place where the unsuspected and often unknown forces of evil take root; forces at the same time impersonal and personal, often unnamable, which superimpose themselves on our being in such an intimate fashion that we do not notice their movements. We are unable to discern whether it is we who act or who are evil, or whether there are alien forces at work in us.

Jesus says in the Gospels that from the heart, all evil thoughts flow. Therefore, the heart should be purified in order to return to its first vocation, which is to be the seat, the throne, the wedding chamber of Christ, wherein is the presence of the Bridegroom. To affirm this does not mean to speak of the heart as a specific place which would exclude all the other faculties of man—mind, feelings, and will—but is aimed to show the heart as the center of convergence and of radiation, as the place of unification of all the faculties, feelings, and living forces of the human being: body, soul, and spirit.

---

[1]Nicholas Cabasilas, *La Vie en Christ*, vols. I and II, ed. du Cerf, coll. "Sources chrétiennes," nos. 355 and 361 (1989 and 1990). [English translation by Carmino deCatanzaro, *The Life in Christ*, St Vladimir's Seminary Press (1998).]

[2]Jean de Cronstadt, *Ma vie en Christ*, ed. Abbaye de Bellefontaine, col. "Spiritualité orientale," no. 27 (1979). [English translation by E. E. Goulaeff, *St John of Kronstadt, My Life in Christ*, Holy Trinity Monastery (2000).]

In this sense, the practice of the prayer of the heart aims not only to this interiority, to this deepest and most radical intimacy with God, when all the rest must be silent, but to render back to us this unity in which the mind is not alien to this intimacy with God. The entire human being moves in the wake of Christ: the body itself prayerfully reflects in its face the presence and grace of God. The tragedy of sin weighs down our civilizations and causes a dissociation in us on various levels of life: autonomy of the senses becomes sensuality; intelligence becomes rationalism; the heart turns toward sentimentality. This break between the mind and the heart, which affects the individual as well as the society, rebounds on Christian culture and society, on behaviors, on the very life of faith. We know how strongly Pascal reacted against that by recalling the predominance, the preeminence, of the reasonings of the heart.

Strong Times and Unceasing Prayer

Our own experience of prayer of the heart is primitive and elementary: instead, we must aim toward the image and likeness of the saints, those able carry out this life program, or to Jesus Christ, our absolute and perfect model. Jesus Christ came to restore the unity of man. In His person, He reveals to us not only God, but also the perfect human being—without fault, without sin, without hatred, just as He left the hands of God. As altogether an image of prayer during His whole life, Jesus presented Himself as turned entirely to God and others. Certainly, the Gospels—Luke in particular—tell us of privileged, isolated moments of Jesus in prayer, preferably at night: at certain solemn moments such as before his baptism in the Jordan; before the institution of the Our Father; before the Passion; or before sending His disciples out to preach.

Having lived our entire human reality, Jesus also experienced moments of strong emotion in which He inwardly was distressed by suffering. In the presence of the dead Lazarus and before the walls of Jerusalem, the holy city that refused the words of the gospel, Jesus wept. He was prey to emotions, to what the Fathers call the "irreproachable passions": the perceptible emotions of the heart when faced by the human condition, not only by human suffering but also by hardened hearts—the greatest, most irrevocable degradation. Suffering includes not only physical or moral suffering but also this compassion of Jesus and of the saints when faced by those who refuse the light, the truth, goodness, and love—explicitly or implicitly, under avowed or disavowed forms. Our prayer must enlarge to the measure and to the image of Jesus.

Isolating moments of Jesus' prayer, however, no matter how rich and important, no matter their proper significance, is misleading: for Christ Himself was altogether prayer—total prayer, prayer of the heart, unceasing prayer. The Father revealed the infinite resplendence of His being, invisible to others, in privileged moments or at the moment of an irresistible appeal to follow Jesus. In His time on earth, every ounce of Jesus' being was familiar with perfect and constant communion with the Father. Such is perpetual prayer: words flow and well up from this incandescence, this mysterious communion. The key to this communion is the Holy Spirit, the one whom St Augustine, together with the entire tradition of the Church, called "the bond of love between the Father and the Son."

The Oblation of the Heart

Being entirely turned toward the Father is to share His love, His infinite compassion for the creature. "God so loved the world that He gave His one and only Son" (Jn 3:16). Jesus—by the very fact that He is one with the Father—is one with us, merciful and compassionate. He fully shares the suffering and needs of people, even taking them upon Himself. Thus, it is proper to emphasize the most intimate and the most "exclusive" times of prayer, whether it be in the private or public life, when the Church gathers together in communion and eucharistic prayer. "One-on-one" moments of the believer with the Holy Trinity are necessary to living a relationship with the Other. Such strong moments in the life of Jesus reveal the love and the will of the Father. For example, at the baptism in the Jordan, John the Baptist (who repeats the words of Isaiah) says the Lamb of God takes upon Himself—or removes from us—the sin of the world, the entire sinful condition of humanity. Sin is not merely a fault or an injury; it is also degradation, loneliness, and suffering. Jesus takes all this upon Himself, and in the end, He dies from it.

Thus, Jesus Christ is our living and permanent reference. There is no other method, no other apprenticeship of prayer than the prayer of the heart. Indeed, there is no true prayer that is not prayer of the heart. As long as the heart does not pray, the human being does not pray. There is no other way than to have recourse to Jesus—not only to find strength in Him, but so that He may come into us; so that He may pray in us; so that it is no longer we who live but He who lives in us. As He is in the Holy Spirit and the Holy Spirit is in Him, so in us, may the Holy Spirit sigh and call, "Abba, Father."

To confront suffering and evil in all their forms is to continue what Jesus has done, to let Him resound and pray in us, being strengthened by the Holy Spirit. The latter not only is the Spirit of victory and the resurrection; prior to that, He is the Spirit of the passion and the Spirit of compassion.

When man follows the path of Jesus, he learns how to offer his own heart. Here we have the most beautiful and most complete offering a human being could make. As long as the heart remains closed, our offerings of things and actions are not yet pleasing to God. The Fathers never cease repeating this, sometimes in a brutal and harsh manner, in the wake of David (notably Psalm 51 [50]), the prophet Hosea (6:6), and of Jesus: "Mercy is what pleases me, not sacrifice. I abhor your sacrifices and burnt offerings: your fasts also, I abhor them" (Mt 9:13 and 12:7).

All our actions, all our works—even the most noble—reach neither others nor God if they are not preceded, accompanied, followed, and interiorized by this oblation of the heart. It is when the heart opens itself, when it ceases being hardened, when it fortifies itself with the spirit of compassion, that it is able to fill itself with the misery of the world. In the prayer of the heart, and in the public prayer of the eucharistic Liturgy, the Last Supper, the Church intercedes for the needs of the world. This intercession must be made in the most

general but also the most concrete manner possible, by evoking surrounding needs and difficulties. There is also continuity, a continuation
of the public Eucharist in the prayer of the heart, which the Fathers view
as an inner Eucharist. The two are indeed of the same nature.

The Example of Andrei Rublev

The theological and spiritual commentary Brother Daniel-Ange has
made regarding the icon of the Holy Trinity by Andrei Rublev, in his
book *L'Etreinte de feu*, illustrates this point. Andrei Tarkovsky's film,
Andrei Roublev, related that this icon had been painted at the time of
the Mongolian invasions that devastated the land of Rus, which filled
the people with fear and dread and with moral as well as material desolation. A disciple of St Sergius of Radonezh, one of the great inspir-
ers and founders of monasticism and of the Russian spiritual renewal
at the end of the fourteenth century, Rublev had been an eye witness
to these invasions and all their horrors. "At the end of the fourteenth
century," Daniel-Ange writes, "Russia is still ravaged by these Tatar
invasions, hearts are petrified with fear, famine roams, the enfeoffed
princes tear each other to pieces. A face stands out engraved by asceticism, calmed by prayer, radiant among all: Sergius the sweet, poor
hermit. He plunges more deeply into the mystery of the Three than in
the dense woods of Radonezh . . . How can his monastery be called
other than the dwelling of the Holy Trinity?"[3]

This radiance of St Sergius and his monastery—perhaps the first
to be dedicated to the Holy Trinity in the history of the Russian
Church—influenced the work of Andrei Rublev, in particular his icon
of the Trinity, made around 1422. What a contrast between this icon
and this epoch marked by war, famine, epidemics, and heaps of smok-
ing ruins! Brother Daniel-Ange wonders, "How were these eyes, who
have seen so many children massacred, innocents tortured, so many
churches devastated, nameless dramas, able to project a light so
serene? These hands must have wiped tears and bandaged innumer-
able wounds: How were they able to paint these faces from which

---

[3]Daniel-Ange, *L'Étreinte de feu. L'Icône de la Trinité de Roublev*, Desclée de Brouwer (1980) 15.

flows such peace? In his icons, how does the anxiety of such an epoch not show through?"[4]

If so many horror scenes had not traumatized St Andrei, it is because, undoubtedly very early, he discovered this face on so many tortured faces (their eyes were gouged as was the custom). Having been washed by the tears of his Lord, his eyes ended up embracing all distress, with a look that was able to understand, to commiserate. This look saves because from it flows an unnamable commodity: the tenderness of God. One of these looks may appease, console, and heal, not because it would be closed to the ugliness and sadness of the world, but because, by contrast, it goes to the end of the horror. These wide eyes of Jesus cried as no one has ever cried, but also granted a luminous forgiveness previously unknown on earth. Rublev's icon of the Trinity casts this ultimate glance on his life, his land, and his people.[5]

"Brother Daniel-Ange helps us to see the price paid for this infinite sweetness that emanates from the icon of Rublev, an opened flower in a landscape so tortured and so desolate. Thus, to discover the face of the Lamb in the bruised faces, is to draw from Him the strength of the consoling Spirit, who will wipe away all tears from their eyes. Even today, when the icon of the Trinity of Rublev has been restored, freed from the metallic covering that concealed it, and from layers of successive paintings that betrayed and deformed it, the Church—as in the fourteenth and fifteenth centuries—gives us this same gift. Today, an entire population is on a pilgrimage to the halls of ancient art in the Tretiakov gallery in Moscow, where the Trinity shines resplendent, lifted out of its original setting—the iconostasis of Radonezh—but exposed without any other protection than its boundless intimacy, to the gaze and the prayers of the people."[6]

Such is the icon of the Trinity and such is any icon: for every icon is an icon of the Trinity, every icon is the icon of the Lord, in His saints, in His angels, in the Mother of God. Every icon brings out this inner image, hidden in everyone and located precisely in the heart.

[4]Ibid.
[5]Cf. ibid., 16.
[6]Ibid.

The face of Jesus—revealed, known, and invoked—corresponds to the watermark overshadowed in the depth of each human being, darkened by refuse and impurities. The one, true icon of Christ is hidden, waiting to unveil itself and radiate throughout the heart of the human being. Freeing this icon creates a correspondence, a dialogue with the authentic icon, Jesus, and not only with Jesus but also—necessarily—with people. The prayer of the heart becomes an interiorized Eucharist.

Alone with God

Three more aspects distinguish prayer. First, all prayer—whether personal, intimate prayer or the liturgical, ecclesial prayer—has an "exclusive" character: a "setting apart" of either the liturgical community or a personal "face-to-face" encounter with God. "Let us now put aside all worldly cares"; Let us lift up our hearts unto the Lord"; "Let all mortal flesh be silent"; and "Let us entrust our entire life to Christ our God," Orthodox Christians sing during the Liturgy. The Lord reminds us, "When you pray, go into your room, close the door, and pray to your Father who is unseen. Then your Father, who sees what is done in secret, will reward you" (Mt 6:6). One should not make a show of prayer. True prayer requires these moments of solitude, of being "alone with the Alone." This solitary dimension, not limited to monasticism, represents a requirement of all prayer, a nuptial path of the human soul toward the divine Bridegroom. This exclusive aspect, called "verticality," always must be remembered because it is sometimes forgotten.

The "Mass upon the World"

Second, all prayer has an "inclusive" aspect, in contrast to its "exclusive" dimension. The pendulum of prayer clearly alternates between these apparent contradictions, and a necessary, deep complement reveals itself. Jesus was turned totally toward the Father but at the same time toward the people. By its own dynamism and an irresistible spiritual requirement, inner prayer tends to become intercession, a supplication for people and for the entire world. Teilhard de Chardin called this phenomenon, "the Mass upon the world."

Totally turned toward the Father, Christ carries and intercedes for the entire world: "Father, I want those you have given me to be with me where I am" (Jn 17:24). We are called to be where Jesus is—at the right hand of the Father—to be seated with Him in the heavens. St Paul often speaks of this in his "captivity" Epistles, Ephesians and Colossians, and in the Epistle to the Hebrews. Likewise, the veneration of the Mother of God recalls and symbolizes this motherly intercession of Christ and the saints: "My dear children," St Paul says, "for whom I am again in the pain of childbirth until Christ is formed in you" (Gal 4:19). On the spiritual plane, the man, like the woman—and in the same fashion—suffers the pains of childbirth for those whom they bring into the world, also for those whom they see moving away from the grace of the house of God. Consequently, the most personal and most profound prayer requires embracing the world, concretely and in an everyday manner, bringing it before God. Carrying the world before God involves carrying suffering, horror, and evil, so that they be burned and exorcised—a process possible only to the extent that the roots of evil, which lie in my own heart, are exorcised and burned in the face-to-face encounter with the Name of Jesus.

The Invocation of the Name

This relationship with the Name of Jesus, which consumes, purifies, and sanctifies, is very important in prayer. The Bible gives an entire meaning, full and symbolic, to the name itself, to the "mystery of the Name"—of the man, of Jesus, of God. The name symbolizes the presence, not theoretical but active: a presence of grace or a presence of hatred and evil. Because of this weighty presence, a pure and "virginal" language avoids unduly naming forces of evil and avoids unduly naming God, unless the latter is done in prayer. Ultimately, prayer is the only manner of naming God. Even preaching about Him may only be done to the degree that continual prayer interiorizes such preaching. Legitimately, naming God is conditional.

The mark of the Christian is that this Name of Jesus has entered his or her life. Neither the Byzantine Fathers, nor the hesychasts of Mt Athos, of Sinai, of Palestine, or even of Egypt—including St Macarius, St Antony, and St Pachomius—invented the prayer of the heart and the invocation of the Name of Jesus. The Acts of the Apostles and the Epistles of St Paul attest that even before the name "Christian" was popularized and made common in Antioch, the believers were "those who at all times invoked the Name of the Lord." Furthermore, the first preaching of St Peter ends, in Acts: "And everyone who calls upon the Name of the Lord will be saved" (Acts 2:21). This "Name of the Lord" is *Kyrios*, the Greek equivalent of the Hebrew "Yahweh," the ineffable and holy Name of God that Jesus Himself inherits, by right. St Peter says that Jesus was "made Lord." The Father no longer solely bears this name "Lord." Jesus partakes fully of this divine lordship and possesses this name as His own title.

The invocation of the name "Lord," referring to Jesus, is a very early prayer. Even before the wide use of the Name of Jesus, the term "Lord" in the Aramaic language, *Maranatha*, or "Come, Lord," is used. Certain modern liturgies reproduce this *Maranatha* or its Greek form—*Kyrie eleison*—without being translated, in the Latin and Western liturgies. *Kyrie eleison* is reminiscent of a time when the prayer of the heart was not the prerogative of specialists, of prayer professionals, but when the entire people of God personally practiced it under very varied forms. The Byzantine Church has taught the importance of the Name of Jesus, of this flamboyant name, which we invoke like a benediction and lay like a blessing on every creature, particularly on the suffering.

The Apostolic Dimension of Prayer

The third aspect of the prayer of the heart, of all public or private prayers, is "the apostolic dimension." "One-to-one" entreaty is not sufficient; nor is it sufficient to bring before God all the needs, miseries, and burdens of the world. It is necessary to extricate ourselves from this "face-to-face" encounter, to come down from Tabor, to leave our churches, and to enter into the world like the apostles: "I send you into the world; you are not of this world" (Jn 17:18); and "Go, preach to all the nations" (see Mt 28:19). This latter commandment signifies a preaching that is a life-giving testimony to the Name of the Lord, to the Name that saves, to the Name of Jesus. Consequently, the dismissal of the faithful at the end of the Liturgy has a deep symbolic meaning: it announces the end merely of the first part of the Liturgy. At that moment, the believers enter and bring to the world the presence and the living word of Christ.

Are Newspapers a Help in Prayer?

When faced with the suffering of the world, Archimandrite Sophrony illustrated well the question of prayer in a passage devoted to St Silouan,[7] a monk who lived from 1892 to 1938 on Mt Athos. Staretz Silouan left us a personal, intimate journal which resonates widely in our Western countries and which has been translated into many languages.

One day, during a discussion among the monks, a father confessor related what he had just read in the newspaper and asked Staretz Silouan what he thought of it. The latter replied:

"*Batioushka*, I don't care for newspapers with their news."

"Why not?"

"Because reading newspapers clouds the mind and hinders pure prayer."

"How odd," said the father confessor. "For my part I find just the contrary—newspapers help me to pray. We live here in the wilderness, seeing nothing, and gradually the soul forgets the world and becomes shut up in herself. Prayer then slackens . . . but when I read the newspapers I see how it is with the world, how people suffer, and that makes me want to pray. Then, whether celebrating the Liturgy or praying alone in my cell, I entreat God for all mankind, for the whole world."

Staretz Silouan then replied: "When the soul prays for the world, she knows better without newspapers how the whole earth is afflicted.

[7]Archimandrite Sophrony, *Starets Silouan, Moine du Mont-Athos*, Ed. Présence (1973). [English translation by Rosemary Edmonds, *St Silouan the Athonite*, St Vladimir's Seminary Press (1999)].

She knows what people's needs are and feels pity for them."

The confessor asked: "How can the soul know of herself what goes on in the world?"

"Newspapers don't write about people but about events, and then not the truth. They confuse the mind and, whatever you do, you won't get at the truth by reading them; whereas prayer cleanses the mind and gives it a better vision of all things."

"I don't quite see; what are you saying?" said the father confessor in a manner that recalls the interview between St Seraphim and Nicolas Motoviloff: "It is not clear to me; how can one live in the Holy Spirit? Show me this."

In his story, Father Sophrony continued as follows:

"We all waited for Staretz Silouan to reply but the Staretz sat in silence, head bent, not suffering himself to explain in the presence of a father confessor and older monks how the soul can, in spirit, know the life of the world and the needs and tribulations of men when, remote from all things, she prays for the universe."[8]

In other words, he did not want to reveal his own secret: "Gifted with a knowledge of which only a few men are deemed worthy in a century, he did not permit himself to go beyond an allusion." Perhaps he even felt that what he had said was already too much.

Let us end on a few other words of Staretz Silouan: "If you would hold on to prayer, you must love those who offend against you, and pray for them until your soul is reconciled to them, and then the Lord will give you prayer without cease, for He gives prayer to those who pray for their enemies. In prayer, our teacher is the Lord Himself. He who prays aright has the peace of God in his soul. The man of prayer should feel tenderly towards every living thing. The man of prayer loves all men and has compassion for all, for the grace of the Holy Spirit has taught him love."[9]

[8]Ibid. 73.
[9]Ibid. 497.

CHAPTER FIVE

THE ART OF THE INVOCATION OF THE NAME

"Your prayer knows more about it than you do," Victor Hugo wrote. Prayer is indeed a very great mystery. It is the art of arts, the science of sciences, and the place where the identity, or perhaps the nonidentity, of the person is made manifest.

An Ecumenical Dissemination

Philokalia means "love of beauty." This meaningful expression refers to something deeply anchored in Orthodoxy: God, who created the world beautiful and good, is the source of all beauty. Consequently, in the human being, as the image of God, there is an instinct, a need for beauty no less great than the need for truth and goodness. Thus, St Macarius of Corinth and St Nicodemus the Hagiorite in the eighteenth century published a selection of texts by the spiritual fathers from the fourth to the fifteenth centuries—practically to the end of the Byzantine empire—under the title *The Philokalia*, meaning "love of beauty." The first edition of the Greek *Philokalia* appeared in Venice in 1782, and a revised edition appeared almost a century later in Greece. Almost immediately, *The Philokalia* was translated into Slavonic,[1] by a monk of Ukrainian origin, St Paisius Velichkovsky (1722–94), who settled on Mt Athos and then in Moldavia, where he founded the great monastery of Neamts. Paisius had an extraordinary spiritual influence, first in Moldavia, then in Russia, particularly in the high place of *philokalic* spirituality, on the monastery of Optino.

[1]The Russian liturgical language.

The Slavic *Philokalia* of Paisius was revised by St Ignatius Brianchaninov (1807–67) and then translated into Russian and completed by St Theophan the Recluse (1815–94) in a larger edition that was disseminated widely beyond monastery walls. Today there exists a complete—and even amplified—Romanian *Philokalia* due to Fr Dmitru Staniloaë. In the West, it has appeared in various abridged or complete forms in several languages: French, English,[2] and Italian.

The *philokalic* message—the prayer of the heart, the invocation of the Name of Jesus—has proven to extend far beyond the boundaries of Orthodox churches. *The Philokalia* has acquired an authentic, in-depth ecumenical dimension. Additionally, in many places and epochs, the publication of *The Philokalia* has been linked to an entire movement of spiritual renewal, advocating, among other things, a deepening of the inner life by frequent reception of Holy Communion.

The Treasure of Orthodoxy

As an anthology on *hesychasm*, or "stillness," *The Philokalia* on the one hand dictates labor, prayer, and the struggle against the passions and, on the other hand prescribes inner silence, quietness, resting in God. A central theme of interior prayer—beyond the external and liturgical forms of prayer—in search of the inner human being, of which St Paul already speaks (Rom 7:22; 2 Cor 4:16; Eph 3:16), runs through these texts, which are spread out over twelve centuries. The invocation of the Name of Jesus is linked directly to this "prayer of the heart," this *hesychasm*. Various formulas for prayer co-existed or were introduced at intervals to arrive at the most current formula: "Lord Jesus Christ, Son of God, have mercy on me (or on us) a sinner (sinners) [the long version] or "*Kyrie Eleison*, Lord, have mercy" [the short version]. A most intimate treasure of Orthodoxy, the message of *The Philokalia* reaches the universal depths of the human being.

---

[2]In English, the text is available under the title *The Philokalia: The Complete Text, compiled by St Nikodimos of the Holy Mountain and St Makarios of Corinth*, trans. by G.E.H. Palmer, Philip Sherrard, and Kallistos Ware, London, Faber and Faber (1979).

Biblical Roots

The "prayer of the heart" is deeply rooted in Scripture. According to the Bible, the "heart" is at once the seat of spiritual understanding, of the desires, of the *élan* toward God, and of the good and evil passions: "Create in me a clean heart, O Lord, and renew a right spirit within me (*dans mes entrailles*)" (Ps 51 [50]:12). An essential parallelism between the heart and the "me" (*les entrailles*, the bowels) appears in this verse. The latter reveals the entire subconscious and the inner reality of the human being, everything that lives inside without necessarily breaking the surface of awareness. The Prophet Ezekiel states, "I shall remove a heart of stone from their bodies, and give them a heart of flesh" (Ezek 11:19). Here, well before modern medical technology, Scripture mentions a heart transplant!

Deeply linked to "the heart," the invocation of the Name appears as a frequent theme in the Old Testament. The Prophet Joel exclaims, "All who call on the Name of the Lord will be saved," and St Peter repeats this passage at Pentecost (Acts 2:21). One may not debase or sell cheaply the holy Name of God: it has to be pronounced only on one's knees.

The liturgy is not only the public form of the prayer of the people, of the Church. The liturgy also echoes in the depths of the heart, where the human person is the celebrant at an altar of inner sacrifice. God calls us to this inner sacrifice: "Mercy is what pleases me, not sacrifice" (Mt 9:13; 12:7). Numerous Old Testament passages recount God's abhorrence of blood sacrifices because truth and justice do not accompany them. Likewise, St Paul admonishes: "Offer your bodies as a living sacrifice; your body is the temple of the Holy Spirit; and you are this temple" (1 Cor 3:16 and Rom 12:1). The Fathers developed the relationship between the public worship of the Church and this inner worship as a *philokalic* theme.

The Old Testament, the church fathers, and the desert ascetics all assert that this liturgy of the heart must become an unceasing prayer, that ultimately it must coincide with the beating of the heart and rhythmic breathing. Thus says the psalmist: "In my heart I treasure your promises, to avoid sinning against you" (Ps 119 [118]:11); "All night, Yahweh, I hold your name in mind, I keep your law. At midnight I rise to praise you for your upright judgment" (Ps 119 [118]:55, 62).

The Name of the Father

Jesus and the Mother of God summarize the entire content of the Old Testament in the transition to the New Testament. In reference to the prayer of the heart, Jesus first learned to pray according to the tradition of Israel. He went to the synagogue. He accompanied His mother and Joseph to the temple. He partook of the family paschal meals, and from His mouth the Name of God ascended in its various forms: Yahweh, Elohim, and Adonai. Jesus prayed the Psalms. Not only did He read the Law and the Prophets, but He also knew them interiorly. The Name of God lived in Jesus: it was His unceasing, fervent prayer.

According to the Gospels, very early on—but we cannot say when because this time is not temporal—Jesus became aware that God is for Him, the Father. At age twelve, He declared in the temple of Jerusalem: "Do you not know that I must be about my Father's business?" (Lk 2:49). As He taught the doctors of the Law, He instructed Joseph and Mary about His divine sonship. From childhood, the Name of Yahweh that He pronounced alternated with, and was superimposed on, a more personal, intimate name, "Abba, Father."

The Holy Spirit also taught Him the name "Father," since Jesus possessed the Spirit within. St Paul says: "The Spirit Himself intercedes for us with groans that words cannot express" (Rom 8:2); and the Spirit of the Son makes us cry out, "Abba, Father" (Gal 4:6). In this double movement, we pray in the Spirit and the Spirit prays in us. If true for the saints, it is infinitely more so for Jesus. He fully was in the Spirit, and the Spirit was fully in Him.

St Luke's Gospel records the seventy-two disciples' return from preaching: "Lord, even the demons submit to us in your name." Jesus answers them, "Do not rejoice that the spirits submit to you, but rejoice that your names are recorded in heaven." The gospel writer adds: "Jesus full of joy through the Holy Spirit, said, 'I praise you,

Father, Lord of heaven and earth, because you have hidden these things from the wise and learned, and revealed them to little children. Yes, Father, for this was your good pleasure' " (Lk 10:17–21).

In Jesus, prayer was unceasing, perpetual; it embraced the entire space of His heart and being. Jesus is prayer, a prayer concentrated primarily in the Name of the Father. To say "Abba" constitutes Jesus' being one with the Father: "The Father and I are one." (Lk 10:30).

Mary: The Mother of Unceasing Prayer

The life of the Mother of God more fully discloses the secrets of the prayer of the heart. Gregory Palamas (1296–1359) developed a beautiful homily on the Presentation in the Temple, in which Mary enters the space of unceasing prayer. In the Orthodox Church, the Presentation of the Mother of God in the Temple is celebrated on November 21. The feast signifies the coincidence, or rather, the passage from the temple made by human hand to the temple "not made by human hand"—precisely, the Mother of God herself, who carries within the divine Word. Mary is called to become the sanctuary and the temple of God.

According to St Gregory Palamas, Mary, from her entry into the temple, served her apprenticeship in prayer: first the traditional prayer to Yahweh, then the prayer to the Son after the archangel revealed the Name of Jesus. From the Annunciation onward, Mary's entire movement of the heart tended between prayer to God and prayer to the one she carried in her, whose name she knew and murmured in a motherly way—the one to be born, Jesus. In this manner, Mary gradually learned the meaning of her own motherhood by being at the same time turned completely toward her Son and toward God. In her, the Name of Jesus and the Name of God blended. The entire mystery of Mary lies in the unceasing and loving invocation of these two names. Through the grace of the Spirit whose breath penetrated her, these names carried the presence of the Father and the presence of the Son.

The unceasing prayer of Mary was taken up in Romania by a spiritual group called the "Burning Bush" (*le Buisson Ardent*), heirs to the great *philokalic* tradition of the elders of Optino. As a result of their common meditation, this group composed a hymn, the "Akathist of the Burning Bush," of which the final stanza and the refrain are "Rejoice Mary, Mother of unceasing prayer." Here we see how this experience of prayer coincides with the experience of Mary at the very heart of the Church.

The Kenōsis of the Lord

The Lord Jesus communicates to us the Name of the Father: "I have made your name known to them" (Jn 17:26). "I have made you known"—that is, revealed, taught, shared. Jesus shares with His disciples what properly belongs to Him. Only Jesus has the right to call God "Father," but He conveys this right to us, and He gives us the audacity to pronounce it in the Holy Spirit: "And vouchsafe . . . that with boldness and without condemnation we may dare to call upon thee, the heavenly God, as Father, and to say: 'Our Father' . . ."[3] Only by entering into the heart of Jesus can the name of "Father" be truly heard. Discerned in the very heart of Jesus are the groanings of the Spirit. In answer to these words of Jesus, "Abba, Father," the loving voice of the Father is detected: "You are my Son, the Beloved; my favor rests on you" (Mk 1:11); that is, "On Whom rests my entire Spirit," "You are my Son, my Beloved," or simply "My Son," or simply "Jesus."

The invocation of the name of God is inseparable from the mystery of the heart, for there the Name is engraved, the presence of the beloved is lived. We can speak of the heart of God, of the heart of the Father, of His bowels of mercy. In the heart of the Father, the Name of the Son resides, just as in the heart of the Son the Name of the Father resides. Until the agony at Gethsemane and Golgotha, the Name of the Father and that of God are placed upon the lips of Jesus. However, the last cry from the Cross was not "My *God*, my *God*, why have you forsaken me?" (Mt 27:46), but "*Father*, into your hands I commit my spirit" (Lk 23:46).

---

[3]Proclamation of the priest before the recitation by the people of the Our Father in the Orthodox Liturgy.

According to the words of Jesus, the death of the God-man becomes the source of new life: "Unless a wheat grain falls into the earth and dies, it remains only a single grain; but if it dies it yields a rich harvest" (Jn 12:24). However, this *kenōsis* of the Lord, the extreme humiliation of the Suffering Servant, the spotless Lamb sacrificed for the life of the world, reveals His glory that was hidden. St Paul proclaims what may be termed "a Pentecostal rendering of the Name of the Lord" in the christological hymn of Philippians: "And for this God raised Him high, and gave Him the name which is above all other names" (2:9); and He repeats the words of St Peter at Pentecost: "God has made this Jesus Lord" (Acts 2:36). Interestingly, the Septuagint, long before Christianity, translated the term "Lord" (*Kyrios*) for the sacred tetragram, Yahweh, of Israel. The New Testament, especially St Paul, grants Jesus the title "Lord," a name that to us has become almost a banality.

The Prayer to Jesus

In saying, "Our Lord Jesus Christ," we forget all the power and novelty that this title "Lord" had on the lips of the first Christians. Even before being called "Christians" at Antioch, as the Book of Acts relates, they were known quite simply as "those who call on the name of our Lord Jesus Christ" (1 Col 1:2). Consequently, in their deep heart as well as in their collective worship, the first Christians distinguished themselves from Judaism—from which they were not yet separated—through the invocation of the Name of the Lord.

This utterance of two types of prayer, which goes back to Pentecost, contains an extraordinary newness that will last until the end of time. On the one hand, the first Christians continued to go to the temple and address themselves to God, but henceforth gave Him the name of "Father": all collective prayer would be addressed to the Father. On the other hand, simultaneously and through a spontaneous, intimate necessity, they invoked the Name of Jesus directly, not only as mediator, but also as the goal of prayer. Thus, since Pentecost, we pass from the prayer *of* Jesus to the prayer *to* Jesus.

The Meaning of the Kyrie Eleison

There is another invocation important to understanding the liturgy: the Kyrie eleison, "Lord, have mercy." When the Kyrie eleison entered into Christian piety is not well known. Contrary to what is thought, Christian prayer is not a simple refrain to petitions by the deacon in a litany. The Kyrie eleison, properly speaking, *is* the prayer; the deacon gives only the intentions. Unquestionably, the great universal litany that follows the Gospel is an example of this: "Let us all say, with our whole soul and our whole spirit; Kyrie eleison."

The prayer chanted at the Great Compline of Lent, which the priest and the deacon recite during the preparation of the liturgy, is another example: "Have mercy on us, Lord, have mercy on us. Lord, we, powerless sinners, supplicate You. O Master, have mercy on us, have mercy on us, for You are our God, and we are Your people, all of us are the work of Your hands and we invoke Your Name." The significant Kyrie eleison should not be reduced to "a list" (*une kyrielle*). The spirit and the mind cannot follow when the Kyrie eleison becomes merely a list of requests.

A Prayer for All

With further regard to the *Philokalia*, Bishop Kallistos Ware recalls a few basic points in the *Dictionnaire de spiritualité*.[4] He notes first, as Nicodemus the Hagiorite emphasizes in his preface, that the *Philokalia* is a work intended for lay people: it is not reserved for mystics, specialists, monks, and spirituals but is intended for all the Christian faithful. St Nicholas Cabasilas maintains the same in *Life in Christ*:[5] it is not necessary to adopt a particular way of life to lead a full life in Christ; the latter is possible everywhere.

Second, the *Philokalia* links spirituality and dogma, a point that almost has become a triviality for us. Vladimir Lossky has said, "There

---

[4]Bishop Kallistos Ware, "Philocalie," in *Dictionnaire de spiritualité*, fasc. 79 (1984) 1336–52.

[5]Nicholas Cabasilas, *La Vie en Christ*, vols. I and II, ed. du Cerf, coll. Sources chrétiennes," nos. 355 and 361 (1989 and 1990). [English translation by Carmino de Catanzaro, *The Life in Christ*, St Vladimir's Seminary Press (1998).]

is no mysticism without theology; there is no theology without mysticism."[6] A theology entirely separated from the very experience of God would be a dried and desiccated specialization.

Finally, the *Philokalia* aims to show the inner effects of external observations, such as fasting rules. Certainly, we must fast, but Nicodemus writes, "Many Christians are troubled by a multitude of things; by the bodily and active virtues, by the benefits these virtues bring, but they neglect one essential thing: guarding the intellect and pure prayer."[7] Hence, watchfulness, struggle against thoughts, attention, meditation, and spiritual sobriety remain important.

Reading a few texts of the *Philokalia* may give the impression—a wrong one—that prayer of the heart is self-sufficient. People request, "Teach us about hesychasm, and the prayer of the heart." Prayer of the heart is part of a whole, the fulfillment of the commandments, the struggle against the passions, and spiritual asceticism . . . All this takes place in and through the life in the Church.

---

[6]*Essai sur la théologie mystique de l'Eglise d'Orient*, éd. du Cerf, coll. "Foi Vivante" (1990) 7. [English translation, *The Mystical Theology of the Eastern Church* (London: James Clarke, 1957)].

[7]*La Philocalie*, Desclée de Brouwer (1995), vol. I. 38.

CHAPTER SIX

THE INNER EUCHARIST

Our era is more sympathetic to an individualistic conception of salvation or to particular techniques of the prayer of the heart than to ecclesial, cosmic, and social implications. Nonetheless, personal sanctification restores the human being to the liturgical function and vocation to encompass the entire world, the totality of humankind, in a pacified and loving heart. Sanctification restores the liturgical and royal mediation of the human person in a world shot through with waves of hatred and death, obscured by the powers of darkness, a world that groans and waits for the liberation of the children of God (Rom 8:21). Inner transformation of the human heart necessarily restores the sacramental function of the Church, which is to unite all human life to the mystery of the dead and risen Christ and to become transparent to the sanctifying presence of the divine Spirit. The rediscovery of the human being as a liturgical being causes a celebration of praises to God and the inscription of these praises in all modalities of life and work.

The glance cast upon the mystery of Christ—a perpetual, perfect prayer in the fullness of the Holy Spirit—as well as the living Christian tradition, emphasize strongly the inseparable, intimate link between common liturgical prayer, centered on the Eucharist, and the personal rhythms of prayer of the heart. "The Liturgy," Bishop Anastasios Yannoulatos writes, "must be continued in personal and daily situations. Each believer is called upon to pursue a secret liturgy on the secret altar of his own heart, to actualize a living proclamation of the good news for the life of the world. Without this continuation, the ecclesial Liturgy remains incomplete."[1]

[1]Cited by Professor Ion Bria, in "The Liturgy after the Liturgy," *Martyria/Mission, The Witness of the Orthodox Church Today*, Geneva (1980) 67.

Personal Prayer and Ecclesial Liturgy

The entire theological, ecclesiological, and liturgical Orthodox renewal of late cannot be separated from the spiritual movement deriving from *The Philokalia*[2] and of its dissemination among the Orthodox—a renewal to which Fr Dumitru Staniloaë has made a major contribution.[3] Fr Staniloaë gave prominent place to the mystery of the Eucharist in the spiritual space of *The Philokalia*. His conclusions refute the current opinions that distinguish or remove the *philokalic* and hesychast traditions from the practice of the sacrament, particularly the Eucharist.[4] Indeed, he strongly links the ecclesial liturgy with the inward liturgy of the heart, a link rooted in Scripture and found in significant patristic texts. In a remarkable study, Fr Staniloaë writes: "*The Philokalia* attributes a decisive importance to the Eucharistic communion in the framework of the Holy Liturgy of the community, as a means of a person's spiritual growth."[5]

Fr Staniloaë cites St Maximus the Confessor, Callistus, and Ignatius of Xantopoulos, authors of the *Philokalia* who assign a central place to the Eucharist. They speak abundantly of the bread and the wine, not as images of the Body and Blood of Christ, but as the very Body and Blood of Christ. This life-giving Body and Blood form our souls and our bodies. Fr Staniloaë also quotes St Macarius (fourth century): "Just as wine mingles in all the members of the one who drinks it and is transformed in him and he in wine, so does the one who drinks the Blood of Christ quench his thirst with the divine Spirit who commingles with his soul and the soul with Him. For, through the Eucharist, those who commune with dignity reach the ability to partake of the Holy Spirit, and in this manner souls can live eternally."

[2] On the *Philokalia*, cf. chapter 5, "The Art of the Invocation of the Name," of this text.

[3] Not only do we owe him the complete and even expanded publication of the *Philokalia* in Romanian, but the *philokalic* spirit permeates his entire work, beginning with his magisterial doctoral dissertation on St Gregory Palamas published before World War II (1938). This text resumes a conference given in honor of the great theological and spiritual work of Fr Dumitru Staniloaë.

[4] See Boris Bobrinskoy, "La liturgie et la vie de tous les jours," in *Liturgie, Spiritualité, Culture,* Conférences Saint Serge, Rome (1983) 41–52.

[5] See "La liturgie de la communauté et la liturgie intérieure dans la vision philocalique," *Gestes et Paroles dans diverses familles liturgiques,* Rome (1978) 259–73.

From this point of view, it would be appropriate to also quote an amazing third-century text by of the author of the most early *Philokalia*, Origen: "You are, all of you, a priestly people. Consequently, you have access to the sanctuary; each one of you has in himself his holocaust and he himself kindles the altar of sacrifice, so that it burns continually. If I renounce all my possessions, if I carry my cross and follow Christ, I offer my holocaust on the altar of God. If I deliver my body in order to burn with charity, if I acquire the glory of martyrdom, I offer myself as a holocaust on the altar of God. If I love my brothers to the point of giving up my soul for them, if I fight to the death for justice and truth, I offer my holocaust on the altar of God. If I mortify my members of all carnal concupiscence, if the world is crucified to me and I to the world, I offer my holocaust on the altar of God and I become the priest of my own sacrifice."[6]

The fourth-century author, St Ephrem, the founder of Syriac hymnology, already supplies the elements of what will be called *hesychia*, or hesychasm: "[The solitaries] are ordained priests for themselves, and they offer their asceticism. Fasting is their offering and wakefulness their prayer; repentance and faith are the sanctuary, their meditations are the holocaust. Their contemplation is the priest who presides; their lips offer the sacrifice unceasingly, prayer that longs for inner peace."

St Gregory the Sinaite (thirteenth to fourteenth century) summarizes the meaning of the inner liturgy and expresses the spiritual requirement of this descent into the sanctuary, of this immersion in the depths of the heart, and the soberness of the *philokalic* tradition: "The heart freed from all thought is moved by the Holy Spirit Himself and has become a true temple even before the end of time. The liturgy is celebrated entirely according to the Spirit. The one who has not yet reached this state will, thanks to other virtues, perhaps be a good stone in the construction of this temple, but he himself is not yet the temple of the Spirit nor His high priest."

---

[6]Origen, *In Leviticum* 9,9; P.G. 12, 521–522.

Retreat and Silence

The Eucharist and the prayer of the heart—unceasing prayer—are united by common principles. First, both have an "exclusive" aspect: the setting aside of the liturgical community and of the human person for the ecclesial and personal relationship with God. "Let us lay down all earthly cares"; "Let us lift up our hearts unto the Lord"; "Let all human flesh be silent"; "Let us confide our entire life to Christ our God," proclaims the liturgy. Inner prayer requires withdrawal into the cell of the heart, according to the Lord's commandment (Mt 6:6). The monastic enclosure reminds the entire Church of this loving search for the one thing necessary.

The Eucharist, like all private prayer, sets apart the community: "All doors being closed," as the Gospel of John explains. The words of the deacon in early Christianity, "The doors, the doors"—indicating a guarding of the church doors so that no unbeliever would enter during the *epiclesis*—remain with us as a remnant. This exclamation prior to the Creed then did not have a symbolic meaning: it was indeed a matter of closing the doors of the church where only those who communed remained.

Likewise, "Let us lay down all earthly cares," stated at the beginning of the Liturgy of the Faithful and the words sung on Holy Saturday "Let all human flesh be silent" complement the silence before the presence of the Lord. Silence is advocated by the entire spiritual method of the prayer of the heart: to let thoughts be silent in this unique and exclusive face-to-face encounter with the Lord where henceforth everything else is set aside.

Silence deals a deathblow to the intelligence, which flees in fear from it. This is also the meaning of "Let us lift up our hearts" in the eucharistic liturgy. In the Sermon on the Mount, Jesus says: "When you pray, do not do as the pagans do. When you pray, go into your room, close the door and pray to your Father who is unseen. Then your Father, who sees what is done in secret will reward you" (Mt 6:6). The reference is not merely to the inner room of the house, but to the cell of the heart. There are times when this cell must be closed to all external things.

Exorcising the Cosmos

Second, ecclesial prayer and personal prayer have an inclusive, encompassing aspect. Teilhard de Chardin refers to this aspect as intercession for the world, the "Mass upon the World." Christ, turned completely toward the Father, carries the entire world in His filial and royal intercession: "Father, I want those you have given me to be with me where I am" (Jn 17:24). The intercession of the Church is both filial—confident in the love of the heavenly Father—and maternal—it covers and protects the world, symbolized by Marian veneration. Personal prayer cannot elude this obligation to embrace the world and to carry it to God in a general and concrete manner.

During the invocation of the blessed Name of Jesus, a content dark and ambiguous rises from the depths. The heart is purified and freed from the passions and their roots; the forces of evil are exorcised to the extent of the encounter with the Name of Jesus that consumes, purifies, and sanctifies. This deep healing is not limited to the praying individual, but spreads around him or her like a sweet-smelling perfume. Sufferings, pains, preoccupations, and passions good or bad fill the human heart, and they cannot be left at the outer door of the church. If unheeded, these invade us to such a degree that prayer ultimately becomes impossible.

Therefore, it is important to present to the Lord a heart which is "falling apart at the seams" with the misery and the suffering of the world and to purify it and exorcise it. The more the heart is purified and freed from the forces of evil, the more it echoes the suffering found in the heart of the Master who had compassion on the crowds and the sick. Through purification, it images the Master's own heart.

In this way, the most secret, solitary prayer becomes a fervent intercession for the entire world and imitates Jesus, the saints, and the Mother of God. Concerns for this world are laid at the feet of the Savior, in His heart of compassion. Without this method, the weight of the sufferings of all those who come to us would destroy, submerge, and crush us and render us incapable of carrying these burdens. Only in the love of Christ can we descend and remain in the hell or the desert of human hearts and not despair.

Recalling saintly lives explains this process. When Christ appeared to Staretz Silouan, He said: "Keep thy mind in hell, and despair not."[7] Clearly, hell is not only a place "down there," in the depths of the earth, but is also that which arouses the human heart. The heart becomes a hellish place, a place of desolation and despair. We must learn to descend into this desperation, but without despairing—like St Silouan, or perhaps also St Thérèse of Lisieux, who walked along the abyss of unbelief while hanging on to the feet of the Lord.

Metropolitan Eulogius, founder of St Sergius Institute, pronounced a word while giving the monastic veil to Mother Mary Skobtsova.[8] While giving her St Mary of Egypt as her patron saint, he ordered her to go to the "deserts of the human hearts." Deserts or hell—they are about the same. In the Bible, the desert and the night are the abode of evil powers—the same powers that Jesus confronts in those places and times and in hell itself.

Exorcising the cosmos and the depths of the human heart of the satanic powers that operate in us, find shelter in us, and destroy us is done through spiritual warfare, a warfare by Christ Himself, with whom we are integrated in the Eucharist. St Peter says: "Satan is like a roaring lion looking for someone to devour" (1 Pt 5:8). Deep healing, the liberation from these satanic powers, and the victory of Christ spread around the praying individual like a sweet-smelling perfume. This good aroma of Christ enters into and benefits us and those around us. "Acquire a spirit of peace, and thousands will find salvation around you," St Seraphim of Sarov said.

[7]See Archimandrite Sophrony, *Staretz Silouan, Moine du Mont-Athos*, ed Présence (1973). [English translation by Rosemary Edmonds, *St Silouan the Athonite*, St Vladimir's Seminary Press (1991)].

[8]See Mère Marie, *Le sacrment du frère*, Le sel de la terre (1995) 199. [See also chapter three, entitled "Maria Skobtsova," in *Living Icons: Persons of Faith in the Eastern Church*, by Michael Plekon, University of Notre Dame Press (2002)].

The Liturgy after the Liturgy

Additionally, the Eucharist and personal prayer possess an apostolic aspect. The dismissal of the faithful at the end of the liturgy has a profound symbolic and sacramental significance. The *Ite, missa est*, "Go, the mass is ended," of the Roman Mass or the "Let us go in peace" of the Byzantine liturgies announce only the first stage of the liturgy, the "systole" of the Church. This moment marks not just the "exit" from the Church, but also the "entry" of the Church into the world, a continuation of the disciples sent by the risen Lord in the power of the Spirit of Pentecost (Mt 28:18–20; Mk 16:15–20). This other mode of the liturgy, "the liturgy after the liturgy" presents a passage from Sunday, the day of the Lord, to the week. Sunday, as the first of the seven weekdays and at the same time the eighth day, represents a fullness. The entire week, then, becomes an increasingly intense preparation for Sunday. In leaving the church, we carry within the fullness of life in Christ to the world during the entire week. Consequently, the alternating of Sunday and the week is a fundamental principle for the spirit and meaning of the liturgy.

The rhythms of the eucharistic liturgy have been compared to the flux and reflux of the blood in the anatomical heart. There is an alternation between the systole—the contraction of the heart for the expansion of the blood that penetrates the organs, the cells, and reoxygenates them—and the diastole where, on the contrary, the heart becomes larger. When we leave the eucharistic banquet—where the Name of Jesus has become our food and where we are absorbed in Him—the Blood of Christ flows in our veins and irrigates our cells. When our heart beats in unison with the heart of the Master, we are— in the image of the apostles at Pentecost—sent back into the world to announce the wonderful things of God.

Upon the human being nourished by the Word of God and His life-giving Body, the face of Christ is drawn gradually (Gal 4:19), and the emotional life of Jesus is established. Thereby, a person becomes able to carry to people the living Word or, better, becomes a living word permeated by the Spirit. Such a person bestows a look of benediction upon beings and things, of peace, of healing, and of compassion. Such a person, however, also brings into the world the sword of contradiction, the testimony of the crucified Master, the scandalous news of the Resurrection.

As in the Eucharist, the encounter with God in the prayer of the heart must pass into another mode, a mode in which we present God to others. In benediction and with compassion, we lay the Name of Jesus on every creature, our own inner world, and our remembrance of the past and the future. Dom André Louf writes: "As the first Adam, before the fall, was able to give all beings a name that would translate their identity with precision, thus the Christian can, in turn, express in prayer something of 'the new name' which Jesus, the second Adam, gives to all things (Rev 3:12). The new name is enclosed indeed in the Name of Jesus, which we can, like a benediction, lay on everything that passes through our hands, on each human being we encounter, on each face that turns to us. We should touch while we pray, encounter while we bless. In this manner, it is possible to recognize, with Jesus, the new identity of man and of the world. Each of us may have met one day, in our lives, a man of God from whom we received the same gift: his gaze penetrated us like fire, full of the tenderness of God and His purifying power."[9]

The Fruits of the Holy Spirit

Orthodox theology of the sacraments has always given a major role and place to the action of the Holy Spirit: pre- and post-consecratory *epicleses*, constancy of the theme of the communion of the Holy Spirit, vision of the Eucharist as a permanent Pentecost. It is therefore legitimate to establish the place of the Holy Spirit in this inner Eucharist where the prayer of the heart is.

What is the place of the Holy Spirit in the prayer of the heart? Describing prayer of the heart as an exclusively Christ-centered prayer is a basic misunderstanding. Since its inception, the Church has addressed prayers to Christ, of a more intimate character than the great eucharistic prayer, which is always addressed to the Father. But

[9] *Seigneur, apprends-nous à prier*, Lumen Vitàe (1972) 174.

these prayers to Christ constitute, in reality, the Pentecostal turning point, the basic gift of the Spirit: "No one can say, 'Jesus is Lord,' except by the Holy Spirit" (Cor 12:3). Consequently, the motion of the Holy Spirit causes the heartfelt urge to call Jesus "Lord," and to desire His Lordship to live in the heart.

Additionally, the fruit of the prayer of the heart—pronounced as "Lord, have mercy," or "Lord Jesus Christ, have mercy on us" produces the fullness of the gifts of the Spirit. "Lord, have mercy" cannot be reduced to the compassion or pity of a superior Being who looks condescendingly at us. The *Philokalia* clearly attests to the effects of the Kyrie eleison, which carries within all the fullness of the gifts of God.

The *kenōsis* of Christ, His extreme humiliation, resembles a *kenōsis* of the Spirit, because He does not reveal His face or name, but hides Himself. The Spirit engraves in our hearts the Name of Jesus, the icon of Christ, the presence of the Lord. Fr Sophrony in his magnificent little book entitled *De vie et d'esprit* (*Of Life and the Spirit*) notes: "My very dear brothers and sisters, open your heart so that the Spirit may draw in it the image of Christ. You will then gradually become able to have in you joy and affliction, death and resurrection."[10] This reminds us also of the words of St Paul in the Letter to the Galatians: "My dear children, for whom I am again in the pains of childbirth until Christ is formed in you" (Gal 4:19).

Here we touch upon the deep meaning of spiritual fatherhood for those who seek to be awakened to the mystery of Christ through the grace of the Holy Spirit. The mystery of Christ is like a fiery name, a name of blood inscribed in the heart. The Spirit hides from view in the names of Jesus, which He makes present through the invocation of the same name in the heart.

The Word wells up from the inner silence, for we need a moment of silence in the Eucharist as well as in prayer: "It is no longer I who live, but Christ who lives in me" (Gal 3:20). If that is true, even for a moment, it is no longer I who speak, but Christ who speaks in me. "We have the mind of Christ," St Paul says (1 Cor 2:16). "Make yours the mind of Christ" (Phil 2:5). The fruits of the Spirit superabound in

[10] *De vie et d'esprit*, Le sel de la terre (1992) 11.

the "eleison" of the prayer of the heart, the Pentecostal arrival of the Spirit, the mystery of Christ praying in the Spirit.

Jesus prays in the Spirit. He is Spirit. He breathed the Spirit upon his disciples (Jn 20:22). Christ's image develops in us, and we, in turn, pray in the Spirit, as the Spirit prays in us. We become the dwelling place of the Spirit, of His rest. The Spirit makes us Christ—Word, Gaze, Love—and we, in turn well up as streams of living water to the world. "Whoever drinks the water I give him will never thirst. Indeed the water I give him will become in him a spring of water welling up to eternal life" (Jn 4:14). According to Scripture, "if someone is thirsty, let him drink, from his heart shall flow streams of living water" (Jn 7:37–38). In Christ, we are called to be moved by the Spirit, filled with the Spirit, and a source of the Spirit. Such is the mystery, content, and message of the *Philokalia*, of the prayer of the heart lived in the Church.

In his study, Fr Staniloaë concluded by recalling that "Christ is our continuous Pascha. He transfers us unceasingly, in a manner always more perceptible, from the plane of earthly life to the plane of the deified life. He does this mainly through the Eucharist. Moreover, this passage shows in us in our spiritual progress pursued without interruption."[11]

The prayer of the heart constitutes the secret dynamic principle in the reintegration of the entire trend of hesychasm, the entire school of the prayer of the heart, and the entire monastic tradition into the framework of ecclesial life and of common liturgical prayer. Conversely, the biblical authors and the church fathers constantly concern themselves with interior harmonization of liturgical worship and thereby discover the inner roots of the priesthood, whereby each of us is the high priest on the altar of our own hearts who offers the world to God. Discovering the inner roots of the priesthood promotes a sacrificial offering and sanctification of one's own being and results in permanent intercession for the world.

[11]Ibid. 273.

Toward the
Knowledge of God

CHAPTER SEVEN

THEOLOGY AND SPIRITUALITY

All who seek the Lord and wish that their entire being, including their intelligence, be illumined by the light of Christ, live in a constant tension created by a distance separating our daily life—where we have to be—from life with God, of which theology is a reflection.

Theology and spirituality are viewed as two great themes, two domains, two worlds, and two insights as well. One tends to be more intellectual, more theoretical; the other more practical, more lived. We certainly should search for a complement between the two because viewing them as separate entails real dangers. Sometimes the two are opposed; sometimes they ignore one another; sometimes they refuse to acknowledge one another; sometimes they also fear one another. Inaugurating a permanent dialogue between theology—a search for God that structures our understanding—and spirituality—the life in God—is ultimately important, since they must be united.

Silence and the Word

"Theology" is made up of two words: *Theos*, which means "God," and *logos* meaning "word." These two words refer to two persons of the trinitarian mystery: God, the Father, and His Word, the Son. In one sense, the whole of theology derives from the Prologue of the Gospel of John: "In the beginning was the Word and the Word was toward (*pros*, not 'in') God, and the Word was God" (Jn 1:1). Theology as concept, idea, and subject matter contains the mystery of the revelation of God who speaks, of God who utters His Word. "The Word of God wells up from the silence of the Father," St Ignatius of Antioch writes.

Two basic and inseparable concepts, silence and the word, must be compared in speaking of theology. The word, as solely word, becomes chatter; it remains an externalization without depth. Silence, when not expressed, remains inaccessible, as St Paul says, "[He] lives in unapproachable light, whom no one has seen" (1 Tim 6:16). This inaccessible light is the same as silence. The Word of God is the foundation not only of trinitarian theology but also of the universe. God creates through His Word: "God said, 'Let there be light!' " (Gen 1:3).

To speak about God and about the word, and therefore about theology, requires a threefold approach: God in the first person, in the second person, and in the third person.

God in the first person says, "I." To say that God speaks is extremely important, even if we cannot hear the words. God creates by speech, and the Word of God is the essential, ontological act through which the human being and the world came into existence. God carries the world through His Word, which simply does not pass through the air. The church fathers and modern theologians state that the *Logos* (the Word) is the substance of things: all these *logoi*, all these "words," are contained in the eternal Logos, the Son of God. In theological terms, God's words cause a "revelation," a revelation that founds the relationship between the human being and God. God creates the world through His Word. He creates humanity through His word, puts humanity in front of Him, and then dialogues with the human being through His word. In this first stage, the human being listens and accepts in the depths of the heart the Word of God like a seed that must die to germinate and grow. In the presence of God who speaks, first there is listening, second obedience—the "yes," the *amen,* of the human being to God.

Next, let us consider God in the second person. The human being, the angels, and all of nature—"Let everything that breathes praise Yahweh" (Ps 150:6)—address themselves to God by saying "you" in the second person. "We praise you, we worship you, we give thanks to you." The human being, as servant, as a child of God, grows in a filial relationship, a relationship of friendship, unity, and communion with God, the outcome of which is deification. "The height of what is desirable," St Basil says, after enumerating the gifts of grace, "is to become God." A dialogue of prayer, of worship—not only ecclesial, but also inner—structures and defines the true existence of the human person.

As a consequence of this dialogue, we can speak of God in the third person. If one isolates God in the third person, one makes an object of Him, one reifies (*chosifie*) Him: this is the great danger of theology. Theology is then severed from its roots, from its foundation, its framework, from this living dialogue where God speaks and humanity responds. Only within a living relationship may one speak of God.

Confessing the Faith

What does it mean to speak about God? We may wonder about this expression and differentiate between various languages. But all languages frame a communal relationship between human beings— ecclesial or social. At Pentecost, the first action of the apostles was "to testify" before those who came to hear them, to those uninformed and on the outside. "Woe to me," St Paul says, "if I do not preach the gospel" (2 Cor 9:16). Preaching was the first manifestation of the descent of the Holy Spirit on the apostles, whom He had led "to remember" and who made the words of Christ come out of their hearts, where they had been engraved. Starting from there, they were able to speak about Christ and the Father. Such preaching, called "witnessing," according to the words of Christ, could lead to suffering and martyrdom: "You are witnesses to this" (Lk 24:28). Those preparing to enter the baptismal and ecclesial community also made a "profession of their faith," that is, they received, assimilated, and confessed the elements of the Christian faith, a faith in the Father, Son, and Holy Spirit.

The Church supplies catechesis for the adult or the child growing up in the Church. Basic elements of the faith are explained, developed, and transmitted according to the pedagogy of the Church.

One last manner of speaking about God, contained in everything said up to now, is theology. Theology is a formulation in the language of the intellect—but of a purified, sanctified, and ecclesial understanding—of the living encounter with God, of the union to God in Christ. This formulation in concepts and words changes with the localities and epochs. A disciple of Origen, Evagrius of Pontus wrote: "The one who prays is a theologian; the one who is a theologian, prays."[1]

"The One Who Prays Is a Theologian"

What is the meaning of this double assertion? Not only does a balance exist between theological thought and an inner movement of prayer, but prayer also is the priority. "The one who prays is a theologian." Absolutely, the one who prays *is* a theologian in the deepest, fundamental meaning of the term. Prayer in itself, whether we know it or not, whether we are fully aware of it or not, is a personal relationship of the human being to God, the trinitarian God. Prayer is always a movement—otherwise, it is not prayer—an élan, a murmuring of the Holy Spirit in the heart.

According to the Fathers, even the desire to pray already is prayer. St Ignatius of Antioch, that great martyr of the beginning of the second century and a disciple of John the Theologian, says in his *Letter to the Romans*: "There is a living water that murmurs in me, 'Come to the Father' " (vii:2).[2] Likewise, St Seraphim of Sarov says that we do not cease calling upon the Holy Spirit, but when He is in us, we no longer need to invoke Him. In true prayer, it is no longer I who pray, but the Holy Spirit who prays in me.

In the letters of St Paul, two passages—which resemble each other and complete one another—better describe the mysterious action of

---

[1]"Sur la prière," chapter 60, of *De la prière à la perfection*, ed. Migne, coll. "Les Pères dans la foi" 85. Evagrius (345–399) has been condemned for certain propositions by the Fifth Ecumenical Council of Constantinople (553), but his basic work remains and has even been incorporated into the *Philokalia*. [For an English translation of Evagrius, with an introduction and notes, see E. Bamberger, *The Praktikos-Chapters on Prayer*, Cistercian Studies Series 4, Kalamazoo (1958)].

[2]*Les Pères apostoliques* ed. du Cerf, coll. "Foi vivante" (1990) 191. [For an English translation, see William R. Schoedel, *Ignatius of Antioch*, Philadelphia (1985)].

the Holy Spirit in the human heart. "What you received was not the spirit of slavery; you received the spirit of adoption, enabling us to cry out, 'Abba, Father!'" (Rom 8:15). "God has sent into our hearts the Spirit of the Son crying, 'Abba, Father'" (Gal 4:6)!

In the Letter to the Galatians, the Spirit of Christ cries out in us, "Abba, Father!" The word *Abba* is an Aramaic term, found rarely in texts and meaning "father," with a nuance of familiarity and intimacy that brings it close to "daddy." The Jews did not dare call God "Abba." Jesus taught us to do it, for He is the one who revealed to us the name "Father": "I have revealed your name" (Jn 17:6). These two passages in St Paul are related to a passage in the Gospel of Mark, during the agony in the Garden of Gethsemane, where Jesus cries out: "Abba, Father, for you everything is possible. Take this cup away from me" (Mk 14:36).

So closely akin are prayer in the Spirit and the prayer of the Spirit in us, that in reality, it is hard to differentiate between the two. There is no tangible boundary, formal or rational. The two blend, but without a fusion of being with the Holy Spirit.

If "the one who prays is a theologian," it is because—we can say this very humbly—each one of us knows prayer in the Spirit. In moments of true prayer, the grace of the Holy Spirit in the heart of our being causes a longing, a desire, a cry for help, emotion before the beauty of the cosmos, or compassion for the suffering that surrounds us. The Holy Spirit introduces us to communion with the Son, Jesus Christ, in the mystery of the Incarnation—the debasement, humiliation, suffering, and death. He educates us as to compassion, by making us suffer with the Lord. Through the way of the Cross and death, He leads us to the new life and the Resurrection. He opens in us a new space, in which Christ appears with His face, the face of a Man of Sorrows and the face of the Risen One. The two go together because in the body of the Risen One the stigmata of the crucifixion remain as shafts of light. The Lord, to the degree we penetrate into His mystery, raises us toward the Father in an infinite, never-ending ascent.

The saying "The one who prays is a theologian" introduces a genuine theology beyond words and concepts, theological theories, and even dogmatic formulations. These latter act as necessary barriers against danger, on the right and the left, but they themselves are based on this living experience of the trinitarian mystery.

"The One Who Is a Theologian, Prays"

The other half of this saying, ". . . the one who is a theologian, prays," is no longer an assertion but rather a judgmental query, addressed to each of those who strive or pretend to practice "the trade"—the ministry of the theologian. It challenges those who feel that they are vested with the charisms of theological expression, of teaching and of knowledge—for they are charisms, that is, gifts of the Holy Spirit. Every reflection on the mysteries of God and of His works represents a judgment, the outcome of which is staked on whether congruity exists between the word and deed, the speech and action, of the "theologian." Speaking of God in the third person carries the inherent danger of cutting speech off from life, of forgetting about God in the second person and the necessary relationship between dialogue and prayer. Theology then becomes a profession, a dangerous intellectual and conceptual exercise that desiccates the inner life.

When I attended the Institute of Theology at St Sergius in 1944, my spiritual father, who was then dean of students and introduced us into the mysteries of theology, said: "You who enter here, if you are afraid of going on, do not go on. This place is dangerous." To speak about God is to speak of the abyss, of the mystery, of the sacred. The constant burden of the theologian is, and must be, an awareness of inadequacy toward the object of research and reflection—God—in the fear, precisely, that He may become object, the one who is the supreme subject.

Patriarch Athenagoras, who retained rather poor memories of theological discussions, undertook the priestly then the episcopal ministry and was overcome by a vision of unity and love among Christians. About 1960, at the height of his unifying action of Orthodoxy and of Christians, he openly and widely remarked: "We will gather all the theologians and put them on an island, with everything they need. And while they discuss, we will love one another." This anecdotal jest borders on the tragic and reveals the real danger within certain Orthodox circles of divorcing theology and life. The theologian who does not enter the royal priesthood of the Church and priests who neglect theological formation run the same risk. This painful divorce has led to a hardening and friction between the theological world and ecclesial circles. "The one who is a theologian, prays" therefore asserts a question, a vocation, an appeal, and a judgment of the Spirit and of Christ on our lives.

A Call to Repentance

Theological language, abstruse and difficult, causes a certain fear, so people prefer a practical spirituality: love of neighbor, prayer, and a certain silence. However, as I have noted, a sharp boundary between theology and spirituality should not exist. Theology truly is the revelation of the divine Logos, of the Word of God, in a renewed understanding and a living truth. Spirituality—a term which derives from the word "spirit"—might be defined as the life in and by the Holy Spirit. The Spirit vivifies all things, for "the letter kills, but the Spirit gives life" (2 Cor 3:6). In the trinitarian mystery, the Word and the Spirit are always one, associated in the trinitarian mystery and in the work of Jesus Christ. On the one hand, Christ bears the Spirit in His work of salvation, and at the same time, He gives the Spirit. On the other hand, the Spirit leads Christ in His earthly life and at the same time He reveals the Son to us.

What are the basic requirements for a living theology, a spiritual understanding renewed in the Spirit? Four points come to mind.

First, repentance, a *metanoia*, a profound renewal of self is required. The entire being must turn away from a dark existence, renounce the "old Adam" and Satan, and sin—all forms, direct or insidious, of illusion and diabolical seduction. The entire being must tend toward a purification of the heart, since the heart is the center of the human mystery—but also purification of the senses by an asceticism of the body and purification of the intellect by an asceticism of the thoughts. When the intellect is severed from grace, it hardens and proudly asserts itself. With all one's effort, the mind must pass through the mystery of baptism, not the precise moment of child's or adult's baptism, but everything that baptism presupposes: preliminary and lasting renunciation of an old life and the desire for a new life, the sacrament of the death and the life of Jesus Christ. Baptism is the high point, the first stage of preparation and of purification, and at the same time the beginning of the life in Christ.

Thus, the proud mind that counts itself as the criterion of things and of the world must be baptized. This mind must discover silence by entering into the depths of the heart and gradually must be taught by the Holy Spirit who leads with a maternal sweetness into the intimate place where God and Christ, are. When the intellect purifies itself by this descent and attentiveness to God, life springs up from the transfigured heart, and the mind finds new words. Jesus Christ said, "Unless a kernel of wheat falls to the ground and dies, it remains only a single seed" (Jn 12:24). In this parable, the grain is our entire being: we die in Christ, Christ dies in us. New life wells up and all that we are—all that we do, everything we say—acquires a new quality in Christ. My words will no longer be my words; my gaze will no longer be my gaze, but rather the word, the language, the look, and finally the love of Christ.

Being in the Communion of the Church

The second requirement for a living theology deals with Church life. In his work *Eglise, Corps du Christ* (*The Church, the Body of Christ*), Georges Florovsky recalls the words of Tertullian: "*Unus christianus, nullus christianus,*" that is, "an isolated Christian is not a Christian." A person who enters into the life of the Church thereby enters into the Body of Christ, which is the Church, in the mystery of communion. In his Epistle to the Corinthians, St Paul develops this important concept. The Holy Spirit, as the Spirit of communion, incorporates us not only into Christ as Person, but into the totality of the Body of Christ, which is inseparable from the Head. This new life includes our communion with the Body of Christ, where we are nourished by His Body, quenched by His Blood, and vivified by the Spirit who unites us into one body. This "Body" contains not only the eucharistic assembly "here and now," but the Church of all times, of all places—the communion of saints. This point is crucial to our understanding of theology. My theology is not *my* theology, not even that of the group to which I belong. Rather, my theology has been formulated through living experience: the life and suffering of the saints since Pentecost—and even before Pentecost by the patriarchs and prophets—in communion. This communion of the saints implies a communion of faith. This explains why the Orthodox Church does not accept intercommunion, which would make light of this profound unity, what Fr Florovsky calls "ecumenism in time." Communion of faith entails not only attempts to create unity with the dispersed members of churches in our world today, but also constancy in maintaining unity with our church fathers.

This concept of "father" is linked to the concept of Church—our fathers in the faith are called "church fathers." It is linked as well to the general concept of fatherhood. In Orthodoxy, the fathers of the church—discovered through reading and meditation—become real fathers. One feels truly begotten by these authors—be they Philaret of Moscow, Theophan the Recluse, Gregory Palamas, Nicodemus the Hagiorite, Irenaeus of Lyons, the Cappadocians, Symeon the New Theologian, or so many others—and perceives a relationship of fathers to sons or daughters in the faith.

Generally in Orthodoxy, the bond of fatherhood runs very deeply, be it among bishops, priests, confessors, or laypeople who have transmitted the faith, who have engendered others in the life in God. This fatherhood constitutes the very framework of Tradition. In the Tradition, that deposit of faith witnessed to by the gospel, revelation is always transmitted from heart to heart by the living, but also from heart to heart by those who *always* are living. Either a personal encounter or a book encounter may produce the living tradition of the Church, the living tradition of the Fathers. In this Tradition, when engendered by the Fathers, we begin by being little children, which is synonymous with trust, obedience, and receptivity. Gradually we grow up, until we reach "the adult age of Christ," as St Paul says. Then called to exercise fatherhood in turn, we transmit the faith to the coming generations. Just as the transition from childhood to fatherhood is a fundamental law of human biology, so it is a fundamental law of spiritual *bios.*

Feeding on the Scriptures

As to the third point for spiritual living, feeding on the Scriptures, especially the Psalms, which are the basic prayers and which nourished the prayer of Christ Himself, is essential. In growing accustomed to reading them regularly and daily, they become an extraordinary source of knowledge, wisdom, and spiritual sensitivity. Little by little, something awakens in us; we become more attentive and more sensitive.

Before arriving at the mystery of Christ, gaining an understanding of the entire Old Testament behooves us since the Lord said, "Diligently study the Scriptures . . . because they testify about me" (Jn 5:39). Extraordinary prophecies speak about the Passion and the Resurrection of Christ, such as the songs of the Suffering Servant in Isaiah (Is 53): "Like a lamb, He was led to the slaughterhouse"; "They have counted all my bones" (Ps 22 [21]:18). Furthermore, liturgical texts often cite these prophecies. Finally, the Gospels constitute the core. Without exaggeration, they are a genuine sacrament. The Western and scholastic habit of speaking about seven sacraments does not exhaust the meaning of "sacrament." Reading the Gospels puts us in the real presence of Christ, just as an icon does. The Gospels are the four basic "icons" of Christ, and they should be read standing up or kneeling.

To Love in Order to Know

Point four concerns knowledge and love, which in biblical language go hand in hand. When, after the fall, Adam approached Eve and she conceived Cain, Scripture states, "Adam knew Eve" (Gen 4:25). A complete knowledge of body and soul, the union of two who make "one flesh," a single being, represents love.

When I was young, I read St Augustine, the great church father that has marked the West until now. He said that, in order to love, we first should know. That always has shocked me because I would like to say that in order to know, we first should love. Certainly the two go together. St Paul says: "If I speak in the tongues of men and of angels, but have not love, I am only a resounding gong or a clanging cymbal. If I have the gift of prophecy and can fathom all the mysteries and all knowledge, and if I have faith . . . but I have not love, I am nothing . . . And now these three remain: faith, hope, and love. But the greatest of these is love" (1 Cor 13:1–2, 13). He completes this picture by saying: "God has poured out His love into our hearts by the Holy Spirit, whom He has given us" (Rom 5:5). The Holy Spirit pours the love of God into us like an ointment of great price, like a perfumed oil, and this love makes our hearts expand to the extent that God desires.

"Woe to Me If I Do Not Preach!"

Finally, we have an obligation to speak, a duty to witness. The First Letter of St John begins: "What we have heard, what we have seen with our eyes and our hands have touched, that we proclaim concerning the Word of life" (1 Jn 1:1). Nonetheless, we often feel unhappy, for we ceaselessly ask ourselves the question: What is the connection between what we say and what we have seen? What value is there to our words, our language, and our theological synthesis? The human being cannot be satisfied with parceled truth. We search for a vision of the world carried by God, a unified spiritual vision, with all our being, and at the same time, the words we utter—our proclamation to others—always fall short. Fortunately, we have the church fathers and great theologians, and we may repeat things that were expressed and lived better. While repeating them, we try to make all these ideas our own: "Woe to me if I do not preach" (1 Cor 9:16).

Another phrase of St Paul, "For Christ's love compels us" (2 Cor 5:14) testifies to the life in God. This love of Christ in us compels us, pushes us, and forces us not only to do theology, but also to simply be in Christ. Then our silence, as well as our words, will testify to a true theology, prayed and lived.

CHAPTER EIGHT

THE THEOLOGY OF LANGUAGE AND THE LANGUAGE OF THEOLOGY

" The theology of language and the language of theology" is not simple word play, but a matter of a reflection on the theological nature of language and on the status of theology. Dogmas, needed for the faith and for life in the Church, are at once the object of theological formulation and the subject constituting their foundation. Thus, with regard to the Trinity, words concelebrate and praise not only God, but also the Logos and the Father in the power of the Holy Spirit. The word is also christological, divine-human, and sacramental. Lastly, as nineteenth-century Russian religious thought has developed it, the word has, like any human creation, a collegial and communal nature and, thus, ultimately, an ecclesial nature.

The Word of God

Before the existence of the world, God speaks. First of all He speaks in the eternal present of the trinitarian communion, in the eternal generation of the one Son and Word of God. Then He speaks in the timeless instant of the passage from nothingness to being when, through His creative Word, He creates temporality and space. Lastly, He speaks in an absolute word, which does not yet have a partner, before the face-to-face encounter with the creatures, the cosmos, the angelic worlds, and the human being. Thus, the theology of the Word must be founded first on the mystery—simultaneously unfathomable and revealed—of the eternal generation of the Son, the Word of God, inseparable from the Spirit. For it is not possible to think of the Son engendered by the Father without thinking, at the same time, of the procession of the Spirit from the Father and the resting of the Spirit on the Son.

St Ignatius of Antioch, in the second century, wrote, "The Word proceeded from the silence of the Father."[1] Likewise, his contemporary, St Irenaeus of Lyons, wrote, "The Father is the invisible of the Son and the Son is the visible of the Father."[2] Here we have two basic functions of human nature—and therefore divine—which are the word and the image, hearing and seeing. There is a reciprocal relationship between the visible and the invisible, between the image and the prototype, between the word and silence. This fundamental relationship penetrates into the mystery of the word. Not only does the word arise from silence, but it also contains silence and sends us back to the abyss of the mystery of God, beyond all understanding and all words. Silence constitutes the necessary transcendence of the word and its essential reference. The word is not word if it does not refer to a reality beyond itself. That is as true for the symbol as it is for the icon.

In the Prologue to his Gospel, St John writes, "No one has ever seen God; it is the only Son who is close to the Father, who has made Him known" (Jn 1:18). Here we have the silence of the Father, who carries the Son in His eternal bosom and who "speaks" Him in the eternal generation, as Psalm 2 suggests, "You are my son, today have I fathered you" (Ps 2:7). He speaks an eternal word, a word of love, and a word that engenders endlessly. Beyond the word that the Father is, there is the interiority of fatherly silence in the Son Himself: "The Father and I are one" (Jn 10:30). The creative word of the Word wells up, too, from the silence of the Father and carries out the trinitarian plan of creation in the Holy Spirit. Through the revealing words of the Word, God enters into a dialogue with the creature. The dialogue that is established introduces into the ineffable mystery of vision and

---

[1]"Lettre aux Magnésiens," VIII, 2, *Les Pères apostoliques,* ed. du Cerf, Coll. "Foi vivante," (1990) 173. [For an English translation of the letters, see William R. Schoedel, *Ignatius of Antioch,* Philadelphia (1985)].

[2]*Contre les hérésies,* IV, 6, 7, ed. du Cerf (1985) 421. [For an English translation, see *The Treatise of Irenaeus of Lugdunum Against the Heresies,* Society for Promoting Christian Knowledge (1916) 2 vols.].

communion, beyond all language. Thus, the word of God must germinate in the silence of our hearts, in the deepest recesses of our inwardness. There is a link here between the initial and ultimate silence of the trinitarian mystery and the tomb of Christ, that is, death and resurrection. According to the words of Christ: "Unless a kernel of wheat falls to the ground and dies, it remains only a single seed. but if it dies, it produces many seeds" (Jn 12:24).

The creative Word, creating into being from nothingness, acts according to His eternal nature that proceeds from the silence of the Father and manifests the plan of God, the trinitarian counsel. "The Father commands, the Son accomplishes, and the Holy Spirit sanctifies (or vivifies)," the Fathers say. The creative Word keeps the creature in stable well being, not through the outside force of a *deus ex machina*, but from the inside. At the foundation, the indivisible core of created things, are the *logoi*, the reasons for beings, which are contained altogether in the Logos. Philaret of Moscow said: "All creatures are balanced upon the creative word of God, as if upon a diamond bridge: above them is the abyss of divine infinitude, below them that of their own primordial nothingness." The word of God is active to the highest degree in a human being created in the image of God. Isaac of Syria said, "God created man through the Word; the angels he created in silence." The word creates a bond of friendship and establishes a capacity for a common language between the human being and God, a language well beyond our awareness and our intellectual perception. Created in the image of God, the human being's ultimate vocation is to the resemblance inscribed in the first dynamism of human life.

Overturning the Gospel

In the Old Testament, God reveals Himself through His words, His law, His wisdom, and His presence. Through personifications, Judaism tends to relegate God to an inaccessible transcendence by proposing intermediaries between God and humanity. These intermediaries are essential to understand the action of God. For example, he communicates His name—he, the unnamed one. He assumes features of human or cosmic existence, for Scriptures speak of His face: "I have seen God face to face, and have survived" (Gen 32:31), Jacob declares after his vision. Texts also speak about His powerful arm, His divine feelings, His bowels of mercy, His fatherly tenderness, His jealousy, and His anger. Even inanimate things acquire a soul—the rock, the waters, fire or light—and become symbols of life, grace, and the power of God. Human language attributes to God a language and a body to apprehend His mystery of life and of love.

However, the coming of Christ overturns all these evaluations. The Old Testament spoke of God "wearing the light as a robe" (Ps 104:2), but the New Testament speaks of God who *is* light. Whereas the Old Testament spoke of the paternal tenderness of God in the image of human tenderness—"As tenderly as a father treats His children, so Yahweh treats those who fear Him" (Ps 103:13)—the divine fatherhood in the New Covenant becomes primary, and human fatherhood derives from it. St Paul says, "I kneel before the Father, from whom every fatherhood in heaven and on earth takes its name" (Eph 3:14–15). This reversal, however, does not belittle biblical, anthropomorphic language, which, far from being a reflection of archaic religious concepts, essentially approaches the mystery of God in whose image the human is created. It is a matter of recovering the familiarity, the intimacy, and the fundamental relationship with God. The human partakes of this primary mystery of God.

The heart of the theology of language—the key since the coming of the new Adam—is the divine humanity of Christ. As the dogma of the Ecumenical Council of Chalcedon teaches, the gospel of Jesus Christ, the good news that is Jesus Christ, is accorded to His divinity. St Paul says, "In Him, in bodily form, lived divinity in all its fullness" (Cor 2:9). The language of Jesus is not alien to His corporeality; consequently, His body conveys the fullness of divinity. This means that the body shows this fullness of language.

Thus, the Church really partakes of the divine-humanity of Christ, as the Body of Christ, symbolically termed as the all-sacramental notion of the Church, the Temple of the Spirit. The concept of "sacraments" surpasses the framework of seven sacraments established wrongly in the Middle Ages. In the third century, Origen envisioned two sacraments: baptism and the Word of God. I would add the icon as well (both as a sacrament and having therefore a sacramental function). The Word of God, read, commented upon, mediated, and preached in the Church has a sacramental function and an important liturgical and doxological character.

The Three Modes of the Word of God

Three modes of the Word of God may be differentiated. The first is the Word *of* God, coming from Him, where he speaks in the first person; it is a matter of deep revelation, beyond verbal forms. The second is the word *to* God, where we speak to Him in the second person; this constitutes worship, praise, all forms of public and personal prayer, or the praise of creation: "The heavens declare the glory of God" (Ps 19:2). Last, in third place, comes the word *about* God: preaching, catechesis, theology, testimony, apology, and dogmatic formulation. We then speak of God in the third person, while being aware of the danger of turning God into an object; the risk lies in cutting off this third mode from the first two.

Since *the same words* make possible the dialogue with God and the testimony of the Church, a link must unify these three modalities. Thus, certain formulations of conciliar decrees concerning the trinitarian or christological mystery are found literally in the liturgical praise. Numerous passages from the homilies of St Gregory of Nazianzus (fourth century) on the great feasts were taken over word by word by St John of Damascus (seventh and eighth century) in his liturgical hymns. The latter had no trouble singing what he believed and saying what was chanted. If praise and liturgical prayer are preeminently theological, theology is doxological, meaning it derives from praise and communion. Fr Sergius Bulgakov maintained he had taken his entire theological vision from the bottom of the eucharistic chalice. Fr Cyprian Kern said that singing in the choir was the best school of theology.

The Action of the Holy Spirit

Care must be taken not to separate the Word from the Spirit. The Spirit reposes on the Son, the Word of God, from all eternity. Moreover, this represents the Orthodox response to the Roman Catholic doctrine that presents the *filioque*[3] as the best way of accounting for the relationship of the Son and the Spirit. In accordance with the entire liturgical and patristic tradition, the Orthodox Church maintains that there is no need for a causal relationship between the Son and the Spirit. The Spirit rests on the Son from all eternity.

The Spirit makes the creative word of God to germinate in the initial *tohu-wa-bohu* (chaos). He imprints and makes manifest the image of God, which Christ is, in every human being that comes into the world. He conveys the living Word of God and enables the human heart to receive it. He inspires the sacred authors of the Scriptures who become bearers of the Word. He incarnates the eternal Word in the womb of Mary (Lk 1). He enables the disciples to hear the appeal of the incarnate Word and moves them to follow it. He fills Christ Himself and impels Him to the desert of the temptation and toward the preaching of the gospel. He is a witness to the sufferings of Christ. Sent into the world by the Father and the Son, the Spirit evokes for us the words of Christ, and makes the Lord present in the Church until the end of time. Invoked in the eucharistic *epiclesis*, the Spirit makes Christ present in the eucharistic gifts and transforms the eucharistic assembly into the Body of Christ. The Holy Spirit imprints in our hearts the living Word, making this Word ours and causing it to germinate and produce fruit a hundredfold throughout the dark recesses of our unconscious and subconscious. Lastly, the Spirit makes manifest the image of Christ hidden in us, obscured by our passions, according to the words of St Paul: "My children, I am going through the pain of giving birth to you all over again, until Christ is formed in you" (Gal 4:19). As the pre-eminent iconographer, the Holy Spirit

---

[3]The doctrine according to which the Holy Spirit proceeds from the Father *and* the Son, adding *filioque* ("and the Son") to the affirmation of the Creed of Nicaea-Constantinople, according to which the Holy Spirit proceeds only from the Father.

inspires the iconographer. Without the Spirit, the icon, which is always a new miracle, would not see the light of day.

Such is the incarnational and revelatory function of the Spirit, of the one who does not become incarnate, but who incarnates, penetrates, and vivifies the Divine Word that has become human word and image. When the Word of God, Jesus Christ, becomes ours, He merges in us and we in Him. St Nicholas Cabasilas notes: "Unlike human nourishment we assimilate to ourselves, it is Christ—bread, word, image—who assimilates us and unites us to Him, and carries us along in anticipation of His kingdom."[4] When "it is no longer I who live but Christ who lives in me," Christ quenches me with the gifts of His Holy Spirit: love, compassion, discernment, wisdom, and thus language. This is the mysterious reciprocity of "the two hands of God" that carry us to the Father.

Negative and Positive Theology

The words of St John the Evangelist, "No one has ever seen God; it is the only Son, who is close to the Father's heart, who has made Him known" (Jn 1:18), are at the heart of the divine humanity of Christ and of the tension between the two necessary modes of theology: positive, or *cataphatic,* theology and negative, or *apophatic,* theology.

Connected with apophatic theology is the dogma that God remains unknowable in His essence. The Cappadocian Fathers borrowed the concept of essence (*ousia*) from philosophy. However, later Fathers such as Dionysius the Areopagite, Maximus the Confessor, and Gregory Palamas concluded that even this term was inadequate to speak about God and invented the word "superessence" (*hyperousia*). God is *supersubstantial,* unknowable in His being. God, who is at the same time entirely incomprehensible and totally sharable in His energies, lets Himself be known and seen in His hypostases, particularly in the one of the Son, through the light of the Spirit.

---

[4]Nicholas Cabasilas, *La Vie en Christ,* vol. I, éd. du Cerf, coll. "Sources chrétiennes," no. 355 (1989) 299. [For an English translation, see Carmino J. Decatanzaro, *The Life in Christ,* St Vladimir's Seminary Press (1998)].

Thus, this negative dimension of theology unceasingly recalls—against the rationalists who would reduce the mysteries to what reason can understand—God as beyond any concept, any language. At the same time, God communicates outwardly: in personal, inward, spiritual experience, and in the communal experience of the Church. Spiritual experience does not necessitate subjectivism. By itself, my experience is not the foundation of the knowledge of God and of language. But when it is grounded in the common experience of the Church, without dissociating itself, it is valid, for the common experience of the Church always includes personal experience—that of the saints, of the Mother of God, and of the angels. Within the Church, we "drink" this experience—we receive it, we commune of it in the communion of the Word and in the communion of the consecrated bread and wine, the Body and Blood of Christ.

Thus, the incarnation of the eternal Word means that the eternal mystery of God can express itself forever in human words: simultaneously inadequate to this mystery and true. The redeeming Passion and the Resurrection purify, purge, and free the human language from demonic pride and sinful self-sufficiency. The Ascension and seating of Christ at the right hand of the Father harmonize this word with the eternal mystery, of which we partake. Christ has recapitulated us in Himself, and he has restored human language to its first vocation. Finally, the permanent Pentecost of the Spirit in the Church makes us contemporaneous with Christ and gives the Church "the sure gift of truth" (*charisma veritatis certum*), as St Irenaeus of Lyons said with regard to the office of bishop. The certainty of the truth given by God belongs to the entire Church through the episcopal magisterium.

The Teaching of the Church

Thus we arrive at the teaching of the Church, the divine-human body of Christ and temple of the Holy Spirit. St Irenaeus of Lyons shows how the tradition of the Church remains faithful to itself without addition or diminution: "If languages differ throughout the world, the content of the tradition is one and the same. The churches of

Germany have no other faith and no other tradition; nor do those among the Iberians nor those among the Celts, in the East, in Egypt, in Lybia, nor do those who are established in the center of the world. But, just as the sun—this creature of God—is one and the same in the entire world, so is this light which the preaching of the truth is, shining everywhere and illumining all those who want to come to the knowledge of the truth. The most powerful in discourse among the leaders of the Church will not say anything other than that; nor will the one who is weak in words diminish this tradition. For faith being one and identical, the one who can speak eloquently about it does not have more, and the one who speaks but little of it does not have less."[5] Thus, one cannot add to it or subtract from it.

Having said this, the Fathers greatly reserve investigation into the mysteries. St Hilary of Poitiers[6] radically opposed any speculation, even theological. He refrained from scrutinizing the mystery proper to the Holy Spirit: "In my opinion," he says, "there should not be any discussion about whether He is. He is, since as a matter of fact, He is given, accepted, and obtained." Also, he says: "The guilt of the heretics and blasphemers compels us to undertake what is unlawful, to scale arduous heights, to speak of the ineffable, and to trespass upon forbidden places. And since by faith alone we should fulfill what is commanded, namely, to adore the Father, to venerate the Son with Him, and to abound in the Holy Spirit, we are forced to raise our lowly words to subjects that cannot be described. By the guilt of another we are forced into guilt, so that what should have been restricted to the pious contemplation of our minds is now exposed to the dangers of human speech."[7]

In another text, St Hilary continues: "We have been led from the unsheltered places near the stormy ocean out into the high sea, and, although we can neither return nor go forward without danger, the

---

[5] *Contre les hérésies*, I, 10, 66.

[6] Called the Athanasius of the West, St Hilary of Poitiers defended the Orthodox faith against Arianism in the fourth century and wrote a magistral work entitled *De Trinitate* [For an English translation, see Stephen McKenna, *Saint Hilary of Poitiers The Trinity*, The Fathers of the Church (1954)].

[7] *De Trinitate*, III, 1, Paragr. 2. [English translation by Stephen McKenna, The Fathers of the Church, vol. 25 (1954) 36].

journey that we are to follow offers more difficulty than that which we have already completed."[8] "Force yourself into this secret, and amid the one unbegotten God and the one only-begotten God immerse yourself in the mystery of the inconceivable truth. Begin, go forward, persevere. Even though I know that you will never reach your goal, I will congratulate you for having gone ahead. Whoever seeks after infinite things with a pious mind, although he never overtakes them, will still advance by pressing forward. Your power of comprehension comes to a standstill at this boundary line of the words."[9]

The prayer that concludes the first book of St Hilary's *De Trinitate* states: "O almighty God the Father, I am fully conscious that I owe this to You as the special duty of my life that all my words and thoughts should speak of You. This readiness of speech which You have granted to me can obtain for me here no greater reward than to serve You by proclaiming You, and by revealing to the world that does not know You and to the heretic that denies You what You are, namely, the Father of the only-begotten God. This is, to be sure, only the expression of my will. Besides this, I must pray for the gift of Your help and Your mercy that You may fill the sails of our faith and profession, which have been extended to You with the breath of Your Spirit and direct us along the course of instruction that we have chartered . . . Bestow upon us, therefore, the meaning of words, the light of understanding, the nobility of diction, and the faith of the true nature. And grant that what we believe we may also speak, namely, that, while we recognize You as the only God the Father and the only Lord Jesus Christ from the Prophets and the Apostles, we may now succeed against the denials of the heretics in honoring You as God in such a manner that You are not alone, and proclaiming Him as God in such a manner that He may not be false."[10]

These passages elicit the tension, the constraint—almost the suffering—of St Hilary and the Fathers in general when faced with pressure from heretics who compelled them to give an account of their

---

[8]Ibid., II, 88, McKenna, 42.
[9]Ibid., II, 10, McKenna, 45.
[10]Ibid., I, 37–38, McKenna, 33–34.

hope: a negative constraint of the heretic, which is also a positive constraint of the faith.

The Pitfalls of Theology

An intellectual explanation of the faith necessarily entails several dangers, partly from misuse and distrust of reason. When there is a break between reason and the faith, words run the risk of acquiring a mere relative value. That struck me when Fr Yves Congar—a great Dominican cardinal and one of those most involved in finding a solution to the problem of the *filioque*—declared in 1981 (at the sixteenth centenary of the Second Ecumenical Council) that we are united in praise, adoration, doxology, and silence, but that our "dogmatic formulations are nothing but pious approximations of human language that do not affect the divinity." Given the divine-human quality of theological language and of the Church, such a view is unacceptable to Orthodox Christians. The fear of dogmatism runs the risk of causing a rejection of dogmas.

The second danger, at the other extreme, consists of an absolute confidence in dogmatic formulas presented as being totally adequate to the mysteries. This theological and scholastic rationalism parches the heart; the Fathers, since the fourth century, have never ceased to fight against it and insist on the ineffable mystery of God.

An insufficiency of words and concepts outlines the revealed data, and this may derive from the temptation to immure language in silence. Now, Christian theology has an existential, even soteriological task: to defend the faith, to shape adequate concepts, to expand the natural mind through the waters of baptism, and to lift this natural mind in the ascending movement of the entire Church to the level of revelation, making it partake of the knowledge of God.

The conciliar definitions are at once something acquired forever—the Son "consubstantial" to the Father (Nicaea, 325), Mary truly "Mother of God" (Ephesus, 431), Christ "true man and true God" (Chalcedon, 451), the veneration of icons (Nicaea II, 787)—and markers and stages of reflections that must not be closed. This is seen clearly in the conflict concerning the consubstantiality of the Son and the Father in the fourth century. Refuted by radical Arianism, which maintained that the Word is a creature and that there was a time when He was not, "consubstantiality" was also refuted by the semi-Arians in a subtle, more perfidious manner. Indeed, approximating the conclusions of the Council of Nicaea, they added a single *iota* to the word "consubstantial," thus transforming *homoousia* into *homoiousia* and replacing "identity" with "similarity" of nature. In reality an apparently minute difference ruined the entire Orthodox faith. In his book, *The Pillar and Foundation of Truth*,[11] Paul Florensky did not hesitate to say "consubstantial or death." This is also why the church fathers fought to the death to defend consubstantiality, or the two natures of Christ, or the icon.

Identity of nature or similitude of nature: this is all the difference between the creative Word and the creature. The creature is called to resemblance and is on an infinite path, in an endless ascension. St Gregory of Nyssa (fourth century) said: "Going from beginning to beginning, through beginnings that have no end."[12] This infinite path nonetheless does not ever abolish the border between the Creator and the creature. The *iota* added on by the semi-Arians was a subtle and toxic form of the trinitarian heresy.

Faced by this, Basil the Great (fourth century) searched for a middle ground between rejecting the heresy and prudence with respect to words hallowed at the Council of Nicaea. In his position as a fragile minority, he wanted to avoid the use of the word "consubstantial" for the Holy Spirit; so he replaced it by terms of praise, by doxology, in which he affirmed the *isotimia*—the equality of honor with the Father and the Son—or *synthrony*—the Holy Spirit being on the same throne as the Father and the Son. He was reviled not only by the *pneumatochoi* ("fighters against the Spirit") because of his defense of the divinity of the Holy Spirit, but also by the integrationist Orthodox of the time. Desirous to lead the timid to the faith by expressing the same

[11] *L'Age d'homme* (1975) 503.

[12] *La Colombe et les Ténèbres*, ed. du Cerf, coll. "Foi vivante" (1992) 101. [For an English translation, see Herbert Musurillo, *From Glory to Glory: Texts from Gregory of Nyssa's Mystical Writings* (1961)].

idea by different means, he avoided attributing the term "consubstantial" to the Spirit. Nonetheless his position was recognized and retained by the Council of Constantinople (381) in the creed: "Who with the Father and the Son together is worshipped and glorified."

In his funeral oration delivered one year after the death of St Basil, on January 1, A.D. 382, Gregory of Nazianzus, the minstrel of the Trinity, justified and praised his friend's reservation: "The heretics were on the watch for any plain, clear statement that 'the Spirit is God.' They wanted to banish Basil from the city, and seize the church for themselves. But, by numerous texts taken from Scripture, and by proofs that were not dubious in the least and had the same strength, and by necessary arguments, he so pressed his opponents that they were left without reply. At the time, he deferred using the proper terms, and he asked the Holy Spirit and his true defenders not to be offended by his economy (i.e., prudence) . . . But if anyone would accept me as having been his associate in so many things, I will divulge something unknown to most people. Indeed, when the time had driven us to great distress, he undertook the economy while allowing freedom of speech to me, whom no one would bring to trial because of the obscurity of my name, or would banish from my fatherland, in order that our common preaching might be firmly established through the defense of the one or the other."[13]

The Western difficulty in accepting the trinitarian language coined by the fourth-century Cappadocians derives especially from the translation of the term *hypostasis* into Latin. Two solutions were possible: a literal translation, *substantia*, or a simple transliteration in Latin of the word *hypostasis*. Jerome did not understand the Cappadocians and accused them of tritheism. He writes in his *Letter to Pope Damasus*: "After the Nicene Creed, after the Alexandrine decree with the West equally in accord, I, a Roman, am importuned by the Campenses, that offspring of Arians, to accept a newfangled term, 'three *hypostases*.' What apostles, pray tell me, authorized it? What new Paul, teacher of the Gentiles, has promulgated this doctrine? We asked what three *hypostases* may be supposed to signify. 'Three subsistent persons,' they

---

[13] *Oratio* X, III. *In Laudem Basilii Magni*, PG 36: 585–89.

say. We reply that this is what we believe. The meaning is not enough for them; they demand the word itself, because some bane lies hid in its syllables . . . And whoever says there are three—that is, three *hypostases*—attempts under the name of piety to assert that there are three natures. And if this is so, why are we separated by walls from Arius, being united with him in perfidy? . . . Far be it from our Roman faith. Let not the pious hearts of the peoples imbibe so great a sacrilege. Suffice it for us to say that there is one substance; there are three subsistent persons: perfect, equal, coeternal. Let nothing be said . . . concerning three *hypostases* and let there be but one."[14] One sees the misunderstanding about the meaning and the use of a word that, ultimately, would acquire a new meaning.

The Trinitarian Mystery

The key to trinitarian theology is found in the trinitarian mystery because it is a mystery of communion, of eternal concelebrating in which the human being, by the divine humanity of Christ and the Pentecost of the Spirit, is invited to enter. We are invited to penetrate into this mysterious and inaccessible enclosure through the Ascension and the Resurrection, which are also a resurrection and an ascent of our intelligence, of our entire being. As St Paul says: "God has resurrected you in Christ, and he has made you sit at the right hand of the Father." We too are sitting at the right hand of the Father, as is revealed in the Apocalypse, at the end of the letter to Laodicea: "Anyone who proves victorious I will allow to share my throne, just as I myself have overcome and have taken my seat with my Father on His throne" (Rev 3:21). The mystery of Christ, true God and true man, in whom are hidden the treasures of the divinity, is the key to the trinitarian mystery, of which He is the revelation, in the breath of the Holy Spirit. The Christian language is simultaneously and pre-eminently liturgical and theological, as it expresses and formulates the common spiritual experience of the Church—always an experience of holiness

---

[14]Jerome, *Letter 15, To Damasus, The Letters of St Jerome*, trans. by Charles C. Mierow, *Ancient Christian Writers*, no. 33 London (1963) 71–73.

and of ineffable life—and as it raises us toward the silence of communion. We are then in the image of the disciples of Emmaus who first heard the Lord speak but who understood only at the breaking of the bread, when the Lord disappeared from their eyes, and they found themselves in the silence of communion. This theological language, which has numerous verbal consonances, full of imagery and of great beauty, is the silence of vision, of the union.

The Experience of God

I would like to reply to someone who questioned me as follows: "You speak of experience, of spiritual experience, of the experience of the Church. But of what concern is that to us? How does that correspond to your own experience of God? To what degree does it resemble or partake of the experience of the Church of all times and that of all the saints? Either this experience if real in you and your theology can be constructed, or it does not exist and theology is based on the void."

Certainly, a theology not based on a living experience is empty, vain, and sclerotic, even if the words are true and sound, borrowed from the common experience of the Church. How can I reply? Of what value is my experience? I cannot judge this. But I can say that I want to base myself with my whole being, without dissolving myself, on the experience of the saints: in apprenticeship, in humble discovery, in partaking of this common faith that gradually becomes mine, to such an extent that I no longer know where to put the quotation marks around the words of the saints and my own words—quotation marks are a modern invention, unknown to the Fathers. There is a way of living the words of the Gospel and the words of the saints so deeply that they become my own words, spontaneously, naturally. Thus, I feel that the certainty of the saints is mine. With all my being, I desire that this be so. I live the painful alternation of the presence and the absence of God—who of us can say he or she is entirely in the presence of God? I live the oscillation between, on the one hand, peace and joy in the Holy Spirit and, on the other, dryness, inaneness, and spiritual sterility. I live in the faith, that is, in the hope of things to come, in the certainty that God has loved and saved us and that the grace of God superabounds and works through our weaknesses. The Lord tells St Paul that to speak of spiritual experience is not to look at oneself in a mirror or to hear oneself talk, pray, or preach. St Isaac of Syria writes, "True prayer is when one prays without even knowing one prays." To know that one prays is already a return to self. True prayer, then, is to forget about oneself; praying is turning to God and others in the best possible way

Theological Language

Theological language is concentrated in the mystery of Christ, in the holy Name of Jesus, the Name of the Lord (*Kyrios*), the Name of Christ, and finally in all the names he appropriates to Himself: "I am the way, and the truth, and the life" (Jn 14:6). The eternal Word became flesh in the holy Name of Jesus who ascended to heaven. The ascensional dimension of the Church and of worship relates to language and to the image. On this subject, what I had a chance to write about the icon also applies to the Word of God: "The incarnational foundation of the icon must be enlarged to embrace the totality of the redeeming work of the Savior. Each stage of the work of salvation brings about the ability of matter, and above all, of man himself, to become an icon of the trinitarian kingdom. Indeed, ever since the flesh of Christ (and thus matter itself) have been transfigured in the light and the power of the Resurrection , raised to partake of the divine life in the Ascension, and seated in the Lord of Glory to the right of the majesty of the Father, the creature—henceforth in Christ as principle of our salvation and Head of the Church—has become capable of movement toward divine resemblance. Thus, henceforth language and human art can be baptized in the Church; they can, in the fire of the Spirit, become able to translate for our human senses and our understanding the presence of the divine Trinity in itself and in its saints."[15]

[15]Boris Bobrinskoy, *Communion du Saint Esprit*, éd. Abbaye de Belle Fontaine, col. "Spiritualité orientale," no. 56 (1992) 315.

The language of theology is that of the revelation of God and of worship. It is actualized in the "here and now," the *hic et nunc* of the Church, depending on when the Holy Spirit speaks to the churches and, through the churches, to the world. Nonetheless, we are struck by the continuity and the identity between the languages of the Fathers of old and that of the spiritual masters today. Dumitru Staniloaë, Justin Popovic, Kallistos Ware, Archimandrite Sophrony, John Meyendorff, and so many others, speak the common language of the Church. Beyond the crises of theology and of the image, beyond the Babylonian captivity of Orthodox education and iconography—both have known periods of decadence, where the fullness of the faith and the truth lived under a rock, in liturgical worship, in the inner prayer of the saints—we experience today an important renewal, at the same time biblical, theological, iconographic, and spiritual. In particular, Fr Dumitru and others have brought out the merit of the *philokalic* dimension of this renewal with the meaning of hesychasm, of hesychia, which is similar to silence. This spiritual and *philokalic* renewal enriches the Orthodox eucharistic and liturgical life and, starting from there, all of theology.

Nonetheless, an enormous amount of work remains to be done in Orthodoxy in order to give worship, the liturgy, and the Eucharist their central place as the axis of church life, its collegiality and its structures: to make of the Eucharist the source of theological knowledge, as Fr Sergius Bulgakov maintained; to give to theology its full significance as the formulation of a spiritual experience that is lived and always renewed; to give once more to the Orthodox people a sense of the icon, a sacrament of the kingdom. Thus, we must lead the good fight on all fronts at once, for the future of the Church, of the faith, and of theology and give witness to these beyond the canonical borders of Orthodoxy.

In this respect, we should recall all that we owe to our Catholic and Protestant brothers, be it in the rediscovery of the Bible, the publication of texts by the church fathers, or the liturgical renewal. We should discern and rejoice for every germ and desire for Orthodoxy with our separated brethren. Lastly, we must preserve, in the permanent miracle of Orthodoxy, the balance between unwavering fidelity to the tradition of the Fathers and theological research in which we are instructed directly by the Spirit, according to the promise of the Lord: "The Paraclete, the Holy Spirit, whom the Father will send in my name will teach you everything" (Jn 14:26). We should find a balance between obedience, listening to the fathers of the Church, and the direct listening to the Spirit, through them and through the very basis of this ecclesial experience in which we live.

CHAPTER NINE

SACRED TRADITION AND HUMAN TRADITIONS

The delicate, sensitive topic dealing with sacred Tradition and human traditions arouses reaction because in speaking of Tradition, that is, the very life of the Church, one runs the risk of questioning apostolicity, continuity, and fidelity to origins.

In fact, the concept of Tradition appears as a constituent, essential element of Orthodoxy—and not only of Orthodoxy but also of all Christendom. Even if certain Christian families seem to have rejected the idea of Church or apostolic Tradition in favor of *sola scriptura*, Scripture alone, there can be no Church life outside a certain reality of the Tradition. Consequently, Tradition belongs to the very essence of Christianity. But inside the great Christian family, Orthodoxy refers to it and defines it in a privileged manner.

Questions and Tensions

Internal tensions, which stir "the dough" of our Church around certain questions such as the updating of worship, invite reflection upon Orthodox ecclesial identity and lead to scrutinizing the concept of Tradition. Indeed, Fr Alexander Schmemann, in speaking of a "worship crisis" or a "liturgical crisis" in Orthodoxy, opened up a reflection on this "heavenly reality," the liturgy of which the envoys of St Vladimir to Hagia Sophia in Constantinople in 988 spoke—and about which we like to brag and in which we take immense pride.

Besides a "liturgical crisis," certain ascetic practices (the question of fasting is on the agenda of the future pan-Orthodox council, either for a mitigation, or, at any rate, for its reorganization in the new conditions of the civilization of the modern world), the updating of the various canonical rules on the organization of Church life and of the "Diaspora," and the reflection on the criteria and the modalities for the election of bishops, and so forth, beg our attention.

Numerous internal tensions, particularly between the traditional churches, or the "traditionalist" trends, and the "Diaspora," with all its contradictions and its diversity, as several movements and tendencies force further reflection.

Next, the ecumenical dialogue—in which the Orthodox churches have been involved voluntarily or despite themselves for three-quarters of a century—compels us to render an account of our hopes, to justify the doctrinal position of Orthodoxy, to explain the *raison d'être* of its hierarchical and ecclesial structures, of its episcopacy, its worship, its liturgy, its sacraments, its spirituality, its priesthood, and so forth.

Lastly, the rapid changes of the modern world have caused a gulf, not only in the West but also in the lands of the East, between the secularized world—"from within" and marked by technology, the media, the ecological crisis, and bioethics—and a church still seemingly attached culturally to an outdated civilization and moral norms. Under these conditions, the actuality of the Tradition, its limits and its criteria, is raised more than ever. We cannot escape it.

Social and Psychological Dimension

The concept of tradition extends beyond the framework of Christianity and even of monotheistic religions. All human religions, as well as in political, philosophic, lay, and social ideologies contain it. It manifests itself both positively and negatively in totalitarian regimes and racism, which foster hatred. As a basic dimension of society, it unites all humans in solidarity, in space and in time. One of the elements in tradition is heredity, which is transmitted not only from the outside, in words, but also by some type of atavism, an inner, mysterious trend. Heredity itself can be good or bad, as the Western concept of "original sin" reveals. To say this differently: tradition, as a reality and a dimension proper to human life, concerns not only the spiritual, religious, and ecclesial outlooks, but also sociological and psychological approaches.

From this point of view, tradition cannot be dissociated from religious psychology. In it, we discern aspects—at times, pathological symptoms—of excessive religious conservatism and traditionalism or, by contrast, of progressivism and reformism. These aspects reach ecclesiastic circles and influence reflection on their own identities. Thus, there are reactions in the Church that must be defined, diagnosed, and considered in the light of the passions and of the limitations of the human intelligence and of human "isms," pathologies of the psyche.

Biblical Sources

Having said this, a short biblical reminder better defines the theme of the Christian, Orthodox Tradition. In the Judeo-Christian inheritance, Tradition occupies an essential place. When God appears to Moses for the first time, in the burning bush at Sinai (Ex 3:2ff.), He reveals His Name: "I am: that is who I am," and He commands him to go and free His people from Egypt. When Moses exclaims: "What shall I say?" God answers him: "You must tell the Israelites this, it is the God of your forefathers, the God of Abraham, the God of Israel, the God of Jacob who has sent you to them." This theophany already references the Fathers: "The God of their forefathers"—consequently, there is a spiritual remembrance, which for Moses and his people, is the foundation of their identity.

This theme of remembrance is found in the modern world, in what we could call "the reconstitution of the soul of a people." Looking at Russia in particular, Aleksandr Solzhenitsyn has reminded us that if any population loses and removes from the present the creative remembrance of the past and faithfulness to the Fathers, it is deprived of its true spiritual identity.

Thus, the great biblical figures—the first patriarchs, but also Moses, David, Solomon, or the prophets—were the founders of sacred history: continued revelations, in successive stages, whereby the covenant of God and His people was renewed. In other words, God continues to manifest Himself in history; He creates history by respecting it and by following its detours.

Early on, the people of Israel were conscious of being the possessors and guardians of an inheritance: the God of the Old Testament is "the God of our Fathers, of Abraham, of Isaac, and of Jacob." During the life of Christ, the Jews made constant references to Moses and the prophets. The genealogy of Jesus in Matthew and in Luke has import for the Orthodox Church, which celebrates this heritage on the Sundays before Christmas, Thus, Tradition is placed in a divine-human convergence between, on the one hand, the revelation of God, and, on the other, a renewed fidelity of the chosen people through the covenant.

From the Old Covenant onward, there was an interiorization of Judaic orthodoxy, of worship, of Tradition, of the law, and of sacrifice. Very early on, a conflict occurred between the representatives of the Mosaic Law and the prophetic trend that tends, precisely, to recall the importance of the interiorization of worship and of the Law, the spiritual meaning of the entire Tradition. This type of conflict re-emerges strongly in the Gospels and in the Epistles: first, inside Judaism itself, among Pharisees and Sadducees, Orthodox Jews and Essenes, Mosaic Judaism and Jesus ("You have heard that ... But I tell you" [Mk 5:21]); second, among the young Christian community and Orthodox Judaism, Judeo-Christians, and gentile Christians of whom St Paul and St Peter are the representatives (Cf. Acts of the Apostles and the Letter to the Galatians); and last, between the writings of the Old Testament and those of the New Testament (Jn 5:39). Recall also the Sermon on the Mount in the Gospel of Matthew or the conversation of Jesus with the Samaritan woman: "Your fathers worshiped here or in Jerusalem, but the time is coming and has now come when the true worshipers will worship the Father in spirit and truth" (Jn 4:21–23).

For the Christian, the coming to earth of Christ represents the peak of revelation. He is the reference, at the same time first and last, of all future generations until the end of time. He appears as the one who closes the lineage of the prophets, the one who is the key and the subject of all Scriptures and of the apostolic preaching. As in the conversation with the disciples of Emmaus, He interprets in all the Scriptures what concerns Him: "These are the Scriptures that testify about me" (Jn 5:39). Starting from this, all of sacred Scripture becomes normative for church doctrine, the first link of the apostolic Tradition, inside of which it will develop. We should not forget that Scripture is formed within an oral tradition, which gradually becomes crystallized in the "canon of Scripture," that is, the list of Old Testament and New Testament books solemnly canonized by the Church. From the beginning, the Church was able to select among numerous acts, epistles, apocalypses, and so forth, to discern the ones that were authentic, ecclesial, and those that would become the "apocryphal writings."

But if Jesus is the key to Scripture, the Holy Spirit appears as the one who gives us the revelation of this, who reveals "the code" to us, the use of this key. The Holy Spirit gives us the instinct, the sense of the truth. He sets our hearts aglow and makes us recognize and profess Jesus as Lord.

Trinitarian Interpretation

Here, I would like to propose a trinitarian interpretation of the Christian Tradition because it is not just a human interpretation. As a constituent dimension of the Church, the Body of Christ, this trinitarian interpretation is profoundly divine-human and belongs to the very mystery of the Church: that, in many ways, to the extent that a look at the mystery of the faith must correspond to faith itself. The words of the Lord in the Gospel of John, when He imparts the Holy Spirit upon His disciples, may be used as a guideline: "As the Father sent me, so am I sending you" (Jn 20:21). The word "send," which refers to the Greek *apostello*, expresses well the matter of the apostolicity of the Church, of its missionary dimension in time and space, of the very foundation of its hierarchical structures. But we should penetrate deeper into these words of the Lord, "As the Father sent me." What that means is that Christ Himself is the envoy of the Father; His one apostle. The title "apostle" applies to the Lord Himself. The apostles are the envoys of the Lord, but Christ is the Apostle in whom every mission, each apostolate, each apostolic charism finds its source: "What I say is what the Father has taught me" (see Jn 8:28; 12:5ff.).

Thus, Jesus transmits to us the words of the Father. He is the living Word. He is the living Gospel that He announces to us. St Ignatius of Antioch writes, "He is the Word which proceeded from the silence of the Father."[1] In a remarkable study on the Tradition, resumed in *In the Image and Likeness of God*,[2] Vladimir Lossky introduces an altogether unusual concept about the Tradition and the mystery of the Church: silence. From where does silence come when we speak of Tradition? To explain this, the author cites another passage from St Ignatius of Antioch: "He who possesses in truth the word of Jesus can hear even its silence."[3]

In the writings of St Ignatius of Antioch, the theme of silence appears, on the one hand, as a characteristic, almost as an attribute of the heavenly Father, and, on the other, as an attribute of the bishops. That may seem contradictory, to the extent that bishops are called to announce and bring the living Word to the people. Nonetheless, St Ignatius says that "a bishop is never so much a bishop as when he keeps silence."

"The Tradition is silence," Vladimir Lossky writes. This is not a definition, but a first element of the Tradition. We should hear "even the very silence of Jesus," that is, understand that the words come from an unexpected depth and that they carry in themselves a reality "from beyond." This is true of the entire sacramental life, of all language that is our own; if our language seeks to exhaust our intelligence, it becomes hollow very quickly, at the end of its resources. It is only when it seeks to suggest and to sing about depth rather than exhaust it, that language becomes truly eloquent. "He who has ears, let him hear," Christ repeats. That is the meaning of the parables that introduce us into a mysterious, apophatic reality: "Lord, show us the Father," Philip

---

[1]"Lettre aux Magnésiens," VII, 2, *Les Pères apostoliques*, ed. du Cerf, coll. "Foi vivante" (1990) 173. [For a recent English translation of the letters, see William R. Schoedel, *Ignatius of Antioch*, Philadelphia (1965)].

[2]"La Tradition et les traditions," Aubier-Montaigne (1967) 139–166.

[3]"Lettre aux Ephésiens," V, 2, *Les Pères apostoliques*, 164.

asks Christ, who replies, "Anyone who has seen me has seen the Father" (Jn 14:8–9). One cannot go further. Nonetheless, we are called to go further.

Tradition proceeds from the Father. My first statement: "As the Father sent me, so am I sending you" (Jn 20:21) demonstrates that the words of Jesus turn us toward the Father. This word does not break the silence—not anymore than revelation abolishes the mystery—but introduces us to it. This point is important not only in order not to harden the Tradition, nor to reduce it to language or concepts, nor to enclose it in the product of human intelligence, nor reduce it to an image—iconographic or verbal—but also to always perceive the infinite depth of life, beyond verbal or visual symbols.

The living Word of the Father, Jesus Christ, is the permanent content, I would say, even the *only* content of the Tradition. The latter is the mystery of Christ, dead and risen, which the Church announces and presents as a memorial to the world. This very important point lessens the danger in Orthodoxy to forget that Christ is the subject of its preaching and to cover Him with alluvial deposits and the gilding of time. Thus, we speak of and preach the silence of the Father, the living Word, Christ, who is the living content of the Tradition, but also the Holy Spirit who performs the permanent miracle of the Tradition, the identity of the message over the centuries.

"Thus," Vladimir Lossky says, "Tradition is not the content of Revelation, but the light that reveals it; Tradition is not the word, but the living breath which makes the word heard at the same time as the silence from which it came. Tradition is not the truth but a communication of the spirit of Truth, outside of which the truth cannot be perceived: 'No one can say, "Jesus is Lord," except by the Holy Spirit.' "

One therefore could define the Tradition as the life of the Holy Spirit in the Church, communicating to each member of the body of Christ the faculty of hearing, of receiving, of knowing the truth in the light that is proper to it, and not only according to the natural light of human reason. "Thus," to quote Vladimir Lossky again, "the Holy Spirit constitutes the breath of knowledge, the light of the vision." The Holy Spirit constitutes the living surroundings of the vision of God, of sanctification, of knowledge of the Holy Trinity, at the same time ecclesial and personal.

Here we are at the very heart of the mystery, of the double economy of the Son and of the Spirit, so dear to Vladimir Lossky: the reciprocity of the revelation of the Son by the Spirit and of the Spirit by the Son. On the one hand, the Holy Spirit effects incarnation but is not incarnate; He makes Christ present. From the Old Covenant onward, He creates the very structures of the religious life of the people: the priesthood, kingship, the temple, the rituals, the sacrifices, which still have a preliminary, provisional meaning. Last, in the New Testament, the Holy Spirit creates and crystallizes, in the life of the Church, the ecclesial, doctrinal, canonical, and liturgical structures of the body of Christ, without, however, letting such structures become sclerotic and hardened, which is always the temptation of every human society. On the other hand, and, in turn, Christ sends the Spirit in the Church, the Spirit of truth and of holiness. One cannot, therefore, separate Christ and the Spirit, as one cannot separate the rule of faith and the breath of truth and of holiness.

The Apostolic Tradition

It would be important to proceed further to a new distinction—fundamental for the spirit of Orthodoxy—between the "horizontality" of the apostolic transition, and the "verticality" of the teaching of the Holy Spirit in the Church.

"Horizontality" is that which we can delimit under the concept of apostolic succession, in the broad and full sense of the term: the historic transmission—in time and space—of the faith, of the good news, of life, the apostolate, and the episcopate.

When St Paul says: "What I have received, I passed on to you" (1 Cor 15:3), he puts down the very foundation of the apostolic Tradition. Confronted by heresies, the loss of eyewitnesses, and blurred memories, the Church gradually clarified and defined this concept.

A fundamental contribution came from one of the greatest authors of antiquity, who still belonged to an undivided, united,

Eastern and Western Christianity: St Irenaeus of Lyons, a bishop, and probably martyred in the second century. In his major work, *Against Heresies*, he introduced for the first time the term "apostolic Tradition." He solemnly deepened the explication of this Christian doctrine: "The content of the Tradition is one and the same, no one can make any additions whatsoever to it, nor diminish it . . . The preaching of the Church presents in all respects an unshakable solidity. Preaching remains identical to itself."[4] For Irenaeus, the evangelical and apostolic faith was "neither enriched throughout the ages nor impoverished through human transmission." "Neither enriched throughout the ages" because the Pentecostal revelation constituted, for all times, the initial fullness to which no one could add anything; "Nor impoverished through human transmission" because the Holy Spirit always makes us contemporaries to the history of salvation.

Already in the middle of the second century, St Irenaeus, following the bishops of Rome and Smyrna, proved to the Christians and to the Gnostics that the Church was directed by an uninterrupted chain: "the apostolic succession." He listed the first bishops or popes, showing the continuity of the transmission of the hierarchical power of the sacrament of ordination. Having said this, the apostolic Tradition is not limited to the juridical or canonical succession of the hierarchy; it extends to doctrine and to the Church, since these equally are founded on the apostles.

In fact, in modern usage, the term "apostolic" has wide and varied meanings: it refers not only to what is founded upon the apostles but also to that which—like the faith and the Gospel—must be transmitted and communicated, to that which—like the apostles—is sent to the furthermost bounds of the earth. "You did not choose me . . ." (Jn 15:16). "As the Father has sent me, so I am sending you" (Jn 20:21). The apostle defines himself in function of his apostolic ministry of expansion and propagation of the faith, which guarantees the truthfulness of the faith, doctrine, and life of the Church.

Thus, the living apostolic Tradition is, above all, a transmission. In this transmission, there is, indeed, a double movement. First, there is a

[4] *Adversus haereses, Contre les hérésies,* I, 10, 2, ed. du Cerf (1985) 66.

reception through the ages, through the centuries: we receive, and what we receive becomes a part of ourselves, or rather, we become that which we receive; we assimilate one another, identify ourselves with the content of the Tradition. Next, there is a transmission through us, of what has been received in a chain unbroken to the end of the ages. In this respect, it is appropriate to make another distinction between Tradition as a living transmission and Tradition as the content of the faith.

Spiritual Fatherhood

As a living transmission, the Tradition is the work of the Spirit who inspires the one who transmits, who penetrates into the content of the deposit of the transmitted faith, and who enlightens the one who receives it. This transmission is always of the order of a relationship and of personal progress, of a dialogue from heart to heart, from mouth to ear, of an interiorization. More than a phenomenon, we are faced with a true mystery: spiritual fatherhood.

For the deposit of faith to be transmitted unchanged and unchangeable from generation to generation, to retain its integrity, fullness, and simplicity—such as it has been uttered, carried out, and realized in Jesus Christ—the Holy Spirit must act and allow those who have received it and are in agreement with this life and message faithfully to transmit it. In this sense, the concept of spiritual fatherhood, of spiritual begetting, most appropriately expresses what truly constitutes the nerve, axis, and spinal cord of this living reality of the Tradition—irreducible to the external transmission of a truth or a philosophy.

This theme of fatherhood is very broad, not only in Christianity but also in all forms of religion. Fatherhood is an openness of heart, a submission, a deep welcoming not only of theoretical truths, but also of life itself that is transmitted. Transmission becomes a genuine *experience*. What is transmitted is fire. As long as truths remain on the intellectual, cerebral plane, there will be no chance of transmission because they are aloof and cold. Only that which burns can illumine and kindle the core of a being.

From the outset of Christianity, this theme of fatherhood played a vital role. In his famous pastoral epistles, St Paul addressed Timothy (whose mother he knew), whom he accepted as his own child; he passed on the essential faith of which Timothy, in turn, would become the guardian and the transmitter.

In the Church, various forms of fatherhood exist. Spiritual fatherhood in the narrow sense, which is always personal and unique, refers to the fathers who engender us: in our conversion to the faith, through baptism, in our own spiritual growth, or in the monastic life. They let us pass from spiritual childhood to the adult age, to the maturity of the children of God. Fatherhood in a wider sense, which appears particularly when we speak of the "Fathers of the Church," represents a fundamental element of the Tradition. The church fathers are truly our fathers who beget us in the faith. Through them, on the basis of their teaching—be they the ones who have deepened and formulated it, such as St Irenaeus of Lyons or St Basil the Great, or the authors of liturgical texts that nourish us and truly confirm us in the Christian life—we form ourselves; we are born into and grow in the discovery and certainty of the faith.

Thus, we may have numerous fathers, who remain our fathers on condition that we, in our spiritual growth, not only repeat their words, but also deeply assimilate them. Their teachings become part of us, so that we may reach maturity in Christ and become fathers in turn. In this sense, patristics—the golden chain of the Fathers—does not end. The golden chain of the living Tradition and of its actualization extends beyond the fourteenth century, indeed beyond the eighteenth century; it reaches us today and we become the relays of it tomorrow.

This fatherhood is an essential act of the Holy Spirit, in which the two dimensions meet: "horizontality" and "verticality"; "horizontality" because it is uninterrupted since the first centuries until today and will remain so until the end of time; "verticality" because, beyond all human mediations and pedagogies, God is and remains our only Father, Christ our only Lord, and the Holy Spirit our only physician in the growth of the faith.

The Teaching of the Holy Spirit

Tradition as a living transmission is the work of the Holy Spirit. No transmission would be true and sealed in our own hearts if there were no direct teaching by the Holy Spirit. On this issue, we must speak freely, without the fear of falling into illuminism, which is a danger in all epochs. Without saying anything against the charismatic movement, which I respect deeply and where the gifts of the Holy Spirit are made manifest, I recall simply the danger of illuminism: to favor the direct action of the Holy Spirit to the degree of risking reduction and neglect of the entire ecclesial Tradition of the Church.

That warning being given, the direct teaching of the Holy Spirit is paramount. St John says: "As for you, the anointing [a symbolic term signifying the Holy Spirit] you received from Him remains in you, and you do not need anyone to teach you. But as His anointing teaches you about all things—just as it has taught you, remain in Him" (1 Jn 2:20, 27). These words are unique in the entire New Testament. At first sight, they may seem to contradict the entire idea of Tradition and of listening to the masters, the fathers: to the extent that we are in the Holy Spirit, where the Holy Spirit teaches us truly, it would seem that there is no longer any need for us to listen to one another.

Actually, this is not so. The fact that there is a "vertical" dimension of listening is not opposed to Christian obedience, to submission to our fathers in the faith. On the contrary, the Fathers could do nothing without the Holy Spirit; through them, but nevertheless in a direct manner, it is always the Spirit who teaches us.

This subtle dialectic between the direct action of the Holy Spirit and obedience to the Fathers appears clearly in the story of St Paul. Following his "enlightenment" on the road to Damascus, and after spending three years in Arabia—a stay of which we know nothing— St Paul wanted to return to Jerusalem to meet James and Kephas (Peter), the pillars of the Church at that time. This intervention is very interesting because it reveals that, from the beginning of the Church, two basic moments co-existed: on the one hand, the direct illumination of the road to Damascus where St Paul met the living Christ and was taught by the Spirit; on the other hand, the concern to verify his teaching, his knowledge, his preaching, and his language with the apostles, with the Church.

In this way, the Church lives in the breath and the permanent fire of the Pentecost of the Holy Spirit. If this fire does not set us aglow, then all the truths of the Tradition would forever remain as dead, alien externals to us.

In the Christian faith and life, we should never omit any dimension of the spiritual begetting, whatever the relays of transmission may be: the "father," the "charismatics," those who are "filled with the Holy Spirit." For we have only one Lord: Jesus Christ; one Master: the Holy Spirit; and one Father: our heavenly Father. The more we mature in the faith, the more the apostolic and ecclesial Tradition becomes our own. Then the gospel is accomplished, when Jesus tells His disciples: "I no longer call you servants; . . . Instead, I have called you friends, for everything I learned from my Father I have made known to you" (Jn 15:15).

The Doctrine of the Faith

In addition to Tradition as the transmission of the living faith, that is, of the tradition that is living and on the way, there is also Tradition as content of the faith, as objective faith parallel to our subjective faith, our belief, our fidelity, and our stability in God. Objective faith is basically the mystery of Christ, the revelation of this mystery in Jesus, transmitted by the apostles and the evangelists: the announcement of the good news. This is what St Irenaeus calls "the deposit of the transmitted faith," which has remained unchanged over the centuries. This deposit crystallizes in ecclesial doctrine, a doctrine which we have a tendency to call "orthodoxy" and which cannot be separated from worship, prayer, and adoration. Two dimensions are included in the word "orthodoxy": *doxa* not only means thought, prayer, and opinion, but also glory and praise. Consequently, only to the extent that our praise is true does doctrine emerge from inside the language of Christian worship.

We can go even further: *doxa* is not only the glory given *to* God, but also the glory *of* God. Thus, "orthodoxy" is above all the glory of

God who communicates Himself to us in the life of the Church, that is, the living experience of God, crystallized at the same time in the language of worship and in theological thought.

Theology acquires a genuine objectivity in the dogmas, the definitions of the councils, the teaching of the magisterium, and the authority of the Church. That is very important, for it is there that we touch upon the basic mystery of the Church where the Body resembles the Head, Christ being the Head. The entire Church is divine-human or "theanthropical." In other words, everything in the life of the Church is divine-human: worship, the sacraments, the icon, and theological language, taking into account our approximations. From this point of view, the doctrine of the faith acquires a genuine objectivity; the human word becomes *capax Dei* ("capable of God"), that is, capable of transmitting, carrying, and singing (rather than reciting) the truth of God, His mystery.

The miracle of Orthodoxy is to ensure from age to age, the unity and the concordance of the two dimensions in a tension that is sometimes painful but beneficial and necessary: the apostolic Tradition through time and space and the listening and the direct teaching of the Holy Spirit. Moreover, all this is nothing else than the miracle of the Eucharist, where the Church is situated in a dependency on and expectation of the Holy Spirit—an expectation always renewed by His inspirational arrival—and, at the same time, is in fidelity to the apostolic deposit symbolized by the Creed.

Differences between the Christian Confessions

The transmission of Tradition in time and its direct transmission, horizontal and vertical, are both necessary. Fr Georges Florovsky called the first dimension "ecumenism in time." He did this the moment the ecumenical movement—founded after the First World War—developed an intense activity for the rallying of Christians and emphasized very strongly the unity of all Christians in all places: "ecumenism in space." To signify the importance of Tradition and to react against a conception of an ecumenism exclusively horizontal and therefore flat, Fr Florovsky emphasized that the Church is not only defined in space, but also in time, with respect to our Fathers and the two millennia of Christian life in the communion of the saints.

What differentiates the Orthodox vision of the Tradition from that of other Christian confessions? For Protestantism, if there is a Tradition, it ends with the apostolic age. One of the best Protestant theologians, Oscar Cullmann, has sought to revalue Tradition, while maintaining that it did not go further than the life, the testimony, and the writings of the apostles. Fr Jean Daniélou rebutted this position in the journal *Dieu Vivant*. In fact, the *sola scriptura* (Scripture only) has constituted one of the great affirmations of the Reformation since the eighteenth century. Still, in ecumenical dialogue since 1960, Protestants open to the basic value of Catholicism and Orthodoxy have made a discernable effort to reassert the value of Tradition.

Conversely, in Roman Catholicism, one notices in the Middle Ages a certain tendency to place Tradition above Scripture and to emphasize the fundamental and prime magisterium of the pope. This tendency was formulated at the council of Vatican I and taken over, with certain nuances, by Vatican II, but with a rediscovery of the collegiality of the episcopacy, which is a very noticeable step toward Orthodoxy.

In Orthodoxy, the Tradition is alive. It is a permanent miracle in which the Church does not pretend to possess the truth, but rather is possessed by it. The Church does not hold the truth but manifests it in fullness and in permanence, in a eucharistic relationship, an *epiclesis*, where it invokes the Holy Spirit so that He penetrates the gifts— the bread and the wine—the assembly, and, consequently, the very mouths of those in charge of keeping the Church and the entire people of God in the faith and in truth.

This dimension of the invocation—of the *epiclesis*—of the dependency of the entire Church upon the Holy Spirit, is a reality we forcefully maintain. The entire people of God are found permanently in the influential sphere of the Spirit. Thus, all dimensions of the Tradition converge in the one crucible of holiness, for the possession of the truth is inconceivable without personal and ecclesial holiness. The reality of the truth, known and preserved in the Church, must be defined as the object of the responsibility of the entire people of God. For it is the people that are "holy" and responsible and the guardian of the faith and of Tradition. At least, this is the doctrine of the Tradition in the Orthodox Church, as the Eastern patriarchs evoked it in a famous encyclical of 1848 that replied to the problem of "infallibility" even before it was defined at Vatican I.

Loyalty to the Church

Orthodoxy, as such, does not offer a "recipe" regarding human traditions and their evaluation. Nonetheless, it can offer principles to guide its attitude toward Tradition and traditionalism.

First, there is the desire to be faithful to the Church, to its apostolic doctrine transmitted by its hierarchy and by those who have received the charism and the function of teaching, of engendering in the faith. This fidelity to the Church is primary. This is what we maintain in the Creed: not only "I believe" from inside the Church, but also "I believe in the Church." The Church is the very continuation of the mystery of the divine-humanity, that is, of salvation in Christ.

In the Orthodox vision, it is not only inside the Church that Tradition is true and alive. As Irenaeus says: "For this gift of Christ has been entrusted to the Church, and the means of communion with Christ has been distributed throughout it, that is, the Holy Spirit. For where the Church is, there is the Spirit of God; and where the Spirit of God is there is the Church, and every kind of grace; but the Spirit is Truth."[5]

The early Church had a very strong awareness of this particular link between the Spirit and the life of the Church. Particularly, the third part of the ancient creed of the apostles (third century, still in use in the West) unites in one sentence the Spirit and the Church. "I believe in the Holy Spirit in the Holy Church." Certainly, this neither restrains nor reduces the action of the Spirit in the Church. Indeed the Holy Spirit is "present everywhere": He acts in creation; He permeates

[5]Op. cit. III, 24, I, 395.

Christ, fills Him, and orients Him for His mission; and He breathes in the Church.

Second, there is a sense of the mystery, of the beyond, characteristic of the entire dogmatic awareness of the Orthodox Church. This means that the apostolic faith cannot be exhausted in human concepts: there always is a "beyond" to word and language. Thus, in the dogmas themselves—be it the dogma of the divine-humanity of Christ at the Council of Chalcedon in the fifth century, or the trinitarian consubstantiality (the *homoousios*) at the Council of Nicaea in the fourth century—the Church does not seek to exhaust, nor even to define the mystery; it simply wants to place milestones and boundaries, which human thought must be wary of overstepping.

Third, we acquire gradually through our growth and our spiritual maturation the sense, or rather the instinct of truth, which is deposed in the Church.

Fourth, we add, listening to the prophetic Spirit. This is probably the most delicate, the most sensitive if not controversial, point because the Holy Spirit acts in the Church also to awaken us, to thwart the sclerosis of our traditions and of our rites and language to the extent that this language has become repetitive, and to combat the turning of Tradition into traditionalism, in which we cut ourselves off from the expectations and the needs of today's people.

Fifth, there is brotherly love, particularly toward the weak. This charity, to which we must pay attention, is a basic principle of our reflection on the identity of Orthodoxy.

Faced with all this, it must be said that Orthodoxy is at the same time profoundly the same and diverse in the East and the West, be it in Romania or in Greece, in France or in America. It is the same in the sense that we recognize one another—without needing an external authority, a common magisterium that dictates teaching and doctrine—as identical in faith, worship, spirituality, and testimony. It is diverse in the sense that the tonalities of Orthodoxy, its language and preoccupations, may vary greatly from one place to another. To render an account of this, it suffices to compare the existence of the Church in the traditional environments of Eastern

Europe and in the Middle East and in what is still called today "the Diaspora."

The Tradition Questioned

Faithfulness to the Tradition does not mean that it cannot be questioned. Thus, the Fathers sometimes had to act against a certain notion of the Tradition in order to assert the mystery of the faith. For example, when at the Council of Nicaea they had to fight against Arianism, that is, the doctrine that denied the divinity of the Son, it was necessary to choose a term able to express at the same time the one and the three, the unity and the diversity of the three Persons of the Trinity: the word "consubstantial" (*homoousios*). Not being biblical, this term was tainted with heresy because it had been used by the Gnostics and in certain heretical doctrines. Nonetheless, the perceptiveness of the Fathers of the Council of Nicaea allowed the term to be used, in spite of twenty to twenty-five years of conflict that followed, during which the Nicaeans were accused of breaking with Tradition by using terms which neither the Bible nor the Church in its Tradition had known.

The same could be said about the icon. To maintain that the icon contradicted Tradition, the iconoclasts referred in particular to the ban against the use of images in the Old Testament and to its absence in the New Testament.

As another example, starting with the fifth through sixth centuries and up to the eighth century, developing hymnography encountered strong resistance in certain Christian communities, especially monastic communities. The songs, the *troparia*, and the canons seemed to create an imbalance when compared to early worship, which was fundamentally biblical. Up to the fourth and fifth centuries, worship was essentially composed of prayers and the reading of psalms; liturgical chants were relatively few. The extraordinary symphony, the wealth of our liturgical books, almost entirely was composed beginning with the sixth through seventh centuries. The Church accepted and assimilated new forms of Christian and ecclesial meditation on the mysteries of salvation to include them in the traditional "deposit." Even today, on various occasions such as the canonization of new saints in Russia or elsewhere, the Church, moved as it were by an inner need, composes Akathists, songs, and new liturgical texts that do not contradict the Tradition.

From the same evolutionary viewpoint, we may recall that the great feasts such as the Nativity, the Ascension, or those of the Mother of God, were introduced only beginning with the fifth or the sixth century.

Current Problems

Orthodoxy today, at the local and universal levels, in a process of self-reflection, seeks to combine rigorous faithfulness to the apostolic message and the work of the saints to the need for cleansing and purification. Several problems that deal with the Tradition have arisen:

- the canonical discipline of the accession to the episcopacy: until the sixth century, there could be married bishops in the East and in the West;

- the iconostasis that developed and became more massive after the victory over iconoclasm in the ninth century;

- the "secret" prayers during the Divine Liturgy, which are of concern to the entire ecclesial people;

- the partaking of Holy Communion by the faithful: in many places the frequency has diminished and infrequent communion has become the norm;

- the female diaconate, which, in the early Church, was a living, and necessary reality: since the beginning of the twentieth century, the question of reestablishing it has arisen in certain Orthodox regions.

These various examples show that the Church has had, and always will have, to debate the problem of Tradition, which cannot become ossified. It is not a purely theoretical question from which we can escape. The Church concretely must ponder over the actualization of Tradition at the end of the second millennium of Christianity. For this, we must be listening to the Spirit, in whom Tradition and newness are allied, the permanence of the message of salvation and renewal of the ecclesial structures. Only in the Holy Spirit may the complete fidelity to the received Tradition and the most radical freedom of the children of God be realized and maintained without contradiction.

In conclusion, the entire Tradition of the Church is at the same time evangelical, apostolic, and ecclesial: evangelical because the gospel is its source and object; apostolic because it is transmitted by the apostles to the end of time in the totality of space; and ecclesial because the Church is the place, the mode, the discernment, and the authority of the Tradition.

The sole author of the Tradition is the Holy Spirit who acts in synergy, that is, in cooperation with, human freedom. In this living Tradition, fidelity to the teaching of the Fathers of the Church is accepted, loved, and lived as a spiritual bond among all the ages. It is part of the mystery of the Church, which is a divine-human organism: the body of the living Christ. This is why St Irenaeus writes: "This faith, which we have received from the Church, we preserve carefully, because through the action of the Spirit of God, like a deposit of great price enclosed in a good vessel, it rejuvenates ceaselessly, and causes the vessel containing it to renew its youth also."[6]

---

[6]Ibid. [For a recent English version of *Adversus haereses*, see *St Irenaeus of Lyons Against the Heresies*, translated and annotated by Dominic J. Unger, with further revisions by John J. Dillon, Paulist Press (1992)].

SOURCES

"L'Agneau de Dieu prend sur lui la misère humaine," in *supplément au SOP*, no. 89 (June 1984) 13.

"L'amour des enemis dans les Evangiles," in *Buisson ardent, Cahiers Saint-Silouane l'Athonite*, no. 2 (1996) 54–57.

Efficacité du pardon (1993), *pro manuscripto.*

"Entrer dans le pardon de Dieu," *SOP*, no. 186 (March 1994) 25–26.

"La prière du coeur face à la souffrance" (1982), *pro manuscripto.*

"La dimension ecclésiale de la prière du coeur à partir de la Philocalie," *SOP*, no. 176 (March 1993) 24–30.

Prière du coeur et eucharistie, pro manuscripto.

Théologie et spiritualité (1996), *pro manuscripto.*

Théologie du language et langage de la théologie (1994), *pro manuscripto.*

"Tradition sacrée et tradition humaines," *SOP*, no. 147 (April 1990) 20–28.

"La tradition dans le christianisme," in *Fraternité d'Abraham* (1995) 4–8.

INDEX